EVERY STRANGER'S EYES

BEN RANDALL

EVERY STRANGER'S EYES
First published digitally December 2019
Revised for print March 2020, updated August 2020

Content warning:
This story contains references to sexual abuse and violence.

Some names have been changed to conceal identities.
The author does not advocate any methods used herein
to contact or meet with victims of human trafficking.
Vietnamese characters are presented without diacritics.
Prices quoted in the text are given in US dollars,
unless stated otherwise.

ISBN (PDF): 978-0-6487573-0-6
ISBN (Paperback): 978-0-6487573-1-3
ISBN (epub): 978-0-6487573-2-0

Learn more at
www.sistersforsale.com

This book is dedicated to a better future
- for all of us - and to those who are fighting
to make it possible

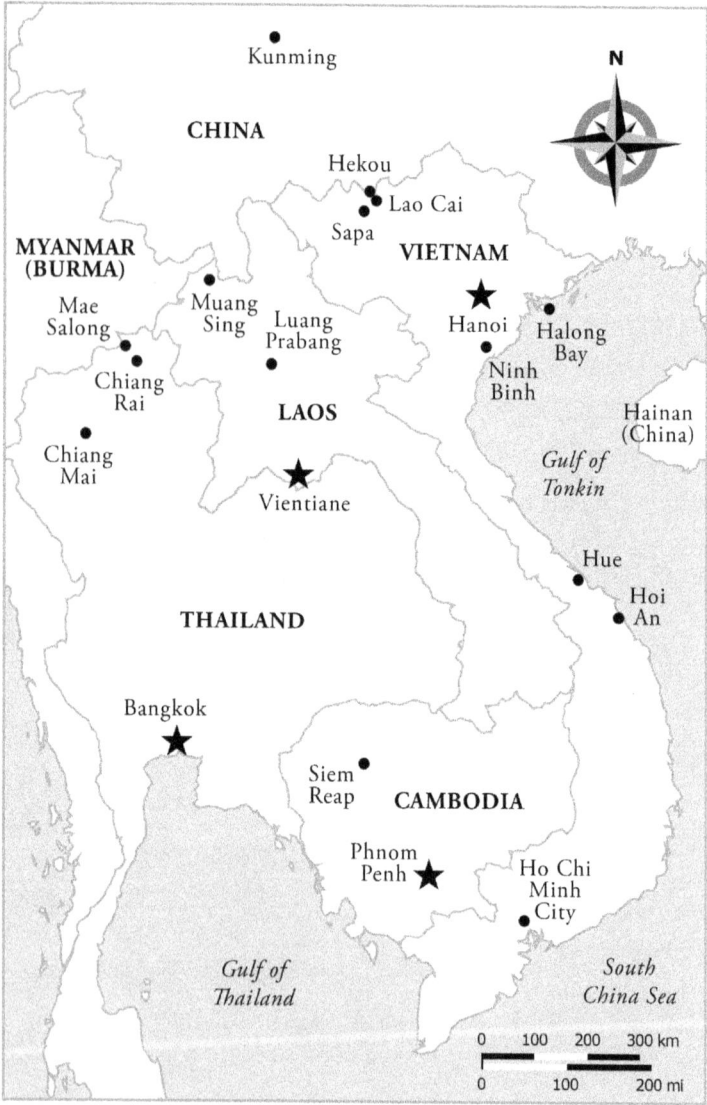

N

Kunming

CHINA

Hekou

Lao Cai

Sapa

VIETNAM

MYANMAR (BURMA)

Mae Salong

Muang Sing

Luang Prabang

Hanoi

Halong Bay

Ninh Binh

Chiang Rai

LAOS

Hainan (China)

Chiang Mai

Vientiane

Gulf of Tonkin

Hue

Hoi An

THAILAND

Bangkok

Siem Reap

CAMBODIA

Phnom Penh

Ho Chi Minh City

Gulf of Thailand

South China Sea

0   100   200   300 km

0   100   200 mi

CONTENTS

"Think. You are alone.
One woman – a slave –
and no help anywhere."

- The Trojan Women,
Euripides

INTRODUCTION

'Every Stranger's Eyes' is the first part of the incredible true story behind the multi-award-winning documentary, 'Sisters for Sale'.

Young women on the border between Vietnam and China find themselves caught between a violent custom and a vicious criminal underworld.

Investigating the mysterious disappearances of his local friends May and Pang, an Australian filmmaker uncovers a human trafficking crisis and sparks an amazing series of events.

Betrayed, kidnapped, and forced into marriage with strangers, May and Pang – still only teenagers – are forced to make the heartbreaking choice between their baby girls and their own freedom.

Since its premiere in Italy in November 2018, 'Sisters for Sale' has won awards and acclaim at film festivals around the world for exceptional filmmaking and courageous storytelling. It has now been translated into more than a dozen languages – an extraordinary feat for such a small production.

'Sisters for Sale' is a five-year story. 'Every Stranger's Eyes' covers the first four of those years, from February 2010 to January 2014.

The second part of the story, 'Suspicious Minds', will be released in mid-2020. A special preview of 'Suspicious Minds' is included in this volume.

The author, Ben Randall, is an Australian activist and acclaimed documentary filmmaker.

His work has been seen and heard by millions of people around the world via new and traditional media - including CNN, Discovery Asia, Newsweek, TEDx, VICE, ABC, CBC, Channel NewsAsia, VTV, Walk Free, Freedom United, Imgur, and Reddit.

The books and documentary are all part of 'The Human, Earth Project', a non-profit grassroots organisation founded by the author in 2013.

All sales help fund the fight against the global human trafficking crisis. Additional contributions make a real difference and are always welcome at humanearth.net.

EVERY STRANGER'S EYES

PART ONE OF THE INCREDIBLE TRUE STORY BEHIND THE ACCLAIMED 'SISTERS FOR SALE' DOCUMENTARY

OUT OF CONTROL

The taxi took me back through a twisting labyrinth of darkened streets. I was somewhere in the endless sprawl of urban China, somewhere between late night and early morning, and I was drunk.

I didn't drink often, and very rarely drank so much, but I'd had an especially good reason that evening.

It had been almost three years since my friend May had been kidnapped from her home in Vietnam, and twenty months since I'd decided to come back to Asia to search for her.

Even before I began, I knew there was no realistic chance of ever finding May – still, I'd let myself hope. I'd come tantalisingly close, further than I'd imagined possible, only to stumble and fall at the final hurdle.

I'd spent months in May's hometown of Sapa, in the northern mountains of Vietnam, investigating her mysterious disappearance. I'd followed a series of scattered clues and false leads thousands of kilometres across Asia, tracking May from the remote villages of rural Vietnam to the glittering megacities of China, where she'd been sold. I'd met resistance in the most unexpected places, and found allies when I'd needed them most.

Incredibly, I'd made contact with May five weeks earlier – but May herself didn't know where she was. Although May had now learned to speak some Chinese, she couldn't read it. The street signs were just as meaningless to her as they were to me.

Using the clues May gave me, I'd narrowed the scope of my search from a vast country of thirteen hundred million people to a circle less than two hundred kilometres across. At the centre of that circle stood a large city, where I'd arrived eight days earlier. May was out there somewhere, not so far away – but so were millions of other people.

May was being held captive in a house somewhere outside the city. She couldn't escape by herself; she'd already tried. May desperately wanted me to find her, to help her out of there, to take her home to her family in Vietnam. I'd beaten the odds and risked my life just to come this far – but it wasn't far enough.

The taxi pulled up outside my hotel, a shabby building near the railway station. The driver turned to me expectantly, and I saw myself through his eyes: a pale, tired-eyed foreigner with a ragged beard and wild hair, in a worn black-denim jacket. Not a knight in shining armour by any stretch of the imagination – but then, May was no princess, either. Only the monster was real.

I passed the driver a handful of coloured notes, and staggered out onto the kerb. The window of my tiny room was just above the hotel entrance. I'd spent the past week holed up in that room, waiting for May's furtive phone calls, scouring the map for any hint of where she might be, trying to stay one step ahead of the man who'd bought her.

"This crazy boy, he very crazy, you know," she'd told me in a phone call a few days earlier, in her broken English. "I was thinking maybe one day he will kill me."

The men who controlled May's life had become aware of my presence, and were doing all they could to stop me from reaching her. May had become concerned for my safety.

"Maybe they take you," she warned. "Not take me, but take you."

I'd called together a team of locals and expats to help me find May – a Texan, a Kashmiri, two Californians, and some of their Chinese friends. It had become a race against the clock, and I'd been forced to make some painful decisions. Whichever path I chose, May would be in danger: I knew that. There was no easy way out for her, not anymore. The best we could do was play the odds – and, if luck was on our side, we might just make the best of a bad situation.

But luck had turned against us, and we'd exhausted

every possibility. I'd done everything I could to find May, and I'd failed.

Earlier that evening, I'd brought the team together and made the grim announcement: after five long months, I was calling off the search. It had just become too dangerous for May. The next day I'd be leaving the area, with no intention of returning. It was a devastating decision, but I was sure it was the right thing to do.

Abandoning a dream is never easy, especially when you've poured so much of yourself into it, and abandoning a friend in her time of need is harder still. I was shattered.

And so we drank. I was glad to have the distraction. I couldn't remember how many bars we'd been to, jagging our way through the city by foot and taxi. It had all become a hazy neon blur as I drank myself into oblivion.

I'd carried my small blue-and-white daypack with me, of course: I carried it everywhere. That daypack contained not only my passport, my bank cards, and all of my most sensitive documents, it held something far more valuable. It held my one last chance to salvage something from this mess.

At home in Australia, I'd worked as a documentary filmmaker. I'd brought another filmmaker to Asia with me, and we'd recorded the search for May to make a feature documentary. If we couldn't help May, I reasoned, at the very least we could share her story, and use it to help other young women in danger.

For five long months, we'd been accumulating

footage of the strange path my search had led us down, and all the people I'd met along the way. That footage was the proof, the undeniable evidence of our incredible odyssey. It had become my most precious possession, the last item of any true value in my life: I'd lost or given away everything else to reach this point.

I'd become extremely protective of that footage, and never let the daypack out of my sight.

The taxi pulled away, and I wove my way across the dark and deserted pavement to the locked hotel entrance. By night there was no doorman, only the key, and the key was in my daypack.

My daypack – that was the moment I realised it was gone. The key was the least of my troubles – *I'd lost the footage.*

For a moment I refused to believe it. It had been painful enough to have lost all hope of finding May. I'd hoped the alcohol would make that easier, but it had only made it worse. Now I truly had lost everything.

I staggered back to the side of the road, collapsed onto the kerb, and sank my head in my hands to stop it from reeling. I tried to make sense of the scrambled mess inside my skull.

Had I left the daypack in a bar somewhere? In a taxi? It could be anywhere by now – where would I even begin to look? How could I be so stupid?

I'd known from the beginning that there wouldn't be a happy ending to this story, but I'd never imagined this.

What did I expect? This was life, and life was messy,

and ugly, and hard. It didn't make sense, and it didn't have to. It never stopped to justify or explain itself, or to reward you for your efforts. Life just rolled on – until one day it rolled right over you, and left you there in pieces.

There was nothing left to do but swallow my pride and admit that the whole thing had been a colossal mistake. It was time to hang my head, tuck my tail between my legs, and begin the long journey back home.

How could this have happened – any of it?

I'd been raised in an ordinary, middle-class family in Australia, where life had been fairly safe and predictable. How did I end up here, drunk and alone on a kerb before dawn in some unpronounceable Chinese city? How did I ever find myself shadow-boxing with organised crime in a land where I couldn't even speak the language?

I'd had a wild idea that I could somehow make a difference, that I could do something good and help somebody, but I could hardly even help myself.

Each of our lives has countless possible paths branching out in countless different directions.

Sometimes we make choices which may seem trivial at the time, but which change our lives completely: we soon find ourselves on new and unexpected paths, moving in directions we'd never imagined. Often, it's only much later that we can look back and see the turning point, the crucial moment where everything changed – and by then, it's too late to find our way back to the world we'd known.

I tried to trace back each step on the path that had led me here, to this country, this city, this kerb.

There was May, of course: she was at the heart of it all. Pang had been a major part of it, too. To trace my steps back to the beginning, I had to go back before Canada and California, before I'd received Zao's message, before my chance meeting with Toan, all the way back to Sapa itself.

It all started on that first day in Sapa – or did it?

Perhaps it began even before that, on that strange afternoon in northern Thailand, when great hidden wheels were already set in motion, turning me in new directions.

It felt like a lifetime ago: it was hard to believe it had only been four years.

ABOUT A GIRL

In February 2010, I was backpacking alone in far northern Thailand, close to the Burmese border.

I'd caught a bus north from Chiang Rai in the hope of reaching Mae Salong, a small town in the hills along the border. Instead, I found myself stranded by the side of a quiet backroad in the countryside, trying to hitch a ride.

It was the middle of a Tuesday afternoon. There was little traffic on the road, and none of it was stopping. I'd been there for an hour or more, and was reading a book while I waited.

A motorbike was coming down from the border region, on the opposite side of the road. I paid it no attention. As it came past me, I heard a sudden strange noise on the road. I looked up to see a local girl lying motionless on her back on the asphalt, just a few metres away.

She looked about fourteen years old. It seemed she'd been a passenger on the motorbike, and had fallen.

I'd been in Southeast Asia for seventeen months at that point. I'd seen plenty of motorbike accidents, and still bore the scars across my back from one of my own – but this was different. The bike had been travelling in a straight line on a level, well-surfaced road in clear, dry weather. There were no other vehicles or objects involved, and it was bizarre that this girl had simply fallen from the back of the bike. There didn't seem to be any reason for it.

It didn't bother me at the time – my first thought was to help the girl. I dropped my book, and stepped into the road.

The motorbike was being driven by a local man in his late twenties. He'd stopped the bike immediately, just a short distance away.

Another man of the same age had been riding a second motorbike not far behind the first. He also stopped his bike, close to where the girl lay. Both men dismounted.

When they saw me approaching the girl, the two men became furious. As they came towards me – one from either side – they began screaming at me in a language I didn't understand, gesturing wildly for me to get away.

I had no idea what the men were saying, but they clearly didn't want my help, so I stepped back.

The two men then turned and began yelling at the girl who lay beneath them. She looked terrified.

I didn't know what to do. What began as a minor traffic accident had suddenly become a socially awkward situation, like seeing a parent strike their child in public. I knew it wasn't right – but was it my place to intervene?

It was another country, another culture. I didn't understand the situation, and couldn't speak the language. I didn't even know which language it was. What could I do? As I hesitated, running through excuses in my mind, the moment passed.

The girl never moved, and never said a word. The men grabbed her roughly, dumped her back on the bike, and rapidly rode away.

Within moments the men, the bikes, and the girl had all vanished down the road. I was left standing there, trying to understand what had just happened.

It had all taken place so quickly – the entire episode had lasted less than a minute. It had been a strange, surreal interruption of an otherwise ordinary day, which resumed the moment the two motorbikes disappeared from view. Nothing remained to show they'd ever been there, and it felt almost as if I'd imagined the whole thing.

I knew human trafficking existed – it existed in an abstract sense, in news reports and magazine articles. It was something that happened to faceless strangers in faraway places, and had no more impact on my own life than an earthquake in Chile, or a famine in Ethiopia. I'd never imagined human trafficking could intrude so suddenly into my life, on a tranquil sunny afternoon in rural Thailand.

And yet, as I turned the incident over in my mind, I could find no other explanation.

It made no sense that the girl had fallen from the bike – and the fact that she'd fallen right there in front of me, on a long and otherwise empty stretch of road, was absurdly improbable. It couldn't have been mere coincidence.

On reflection, it seemed far more likely that the girl hadn't fallen at all: she'd jumped. I was looking for a reason why the girl had come off the bike in that particular place, and I realised that the reason was me.

Wherever that girl was being taken, she didn't want to go – and it hadn't just been a childhood tantrum, either. The girl must have been desperate to throw herself from a moving vehicle onto hard asphalt, especially knowing there was another motorbike close behind.

The girl must have known she risked serious injury, and would only have taken that risk if she'd sincerely believed she was in some greater danger.

I tried to imagine the courage it must have taken in that final moment, to have gambled everything on that one desperate leap from the motorbike. Finding a logical solution to a problem is one thing; risking your own neck to make it a reality is something very different.

It couldn't have been a snap decision. The girl must have been perched there on the back of the bike, waiting and hoping for such an opportunity, for someone who might save her. I was the best she'd found, and I just wasn't good enough.

I couldn't understand why the girl hadn't moved again, after landing on the road. Had she been drugged, injured, or merely terrified? As I tried to imagine myself in her position, I realised there was another possibility. The girl had spent herself completely on her leap from the motorbike. She'd done all that was in her power, and she knew it. Until she'd escaped those men, it was better for her to pretend she'd fallen.

That girl had risked everything on the hope that I could somehow tip the scales and save her. If her desperate gamble didn't work, if I didn't step in to help her, she knew there was nothing more she could do.

She couldn't argue with the men, she couldn't outrun them, and she certainly couldn't fight them. That girl had done everything she possibly could – the rest was up to me.

I'd caught glimpses of the Thai sex industry – it was impossible not to see the barely-legal girls in their miniskirts and spangled bikinis gyrating slowly on the street-side poles in Patong, or luring foreign men into the bars and clubs of Pattaya.

As extensive as it seemed, what was visible to tourists of the Thai sex industry was only the tip of an unimaginably vast iceberg. With a strong local culture of prostitution, the brothels catering to Thai men were much cheaper, more discreet, and far more numerous. The girls there serviced more men, under more horrendous conditions. It was another world accessible only to those who knew which stairs to climb, which doors to knock upon.

I might have been the last thing standing between that girl and a short, brutal life in some squalid Thai brothel. She'd thrown her unprotected body onto the asphalt just to get my attention – and all for nothing.

Not only had I failed that girl, but she'd shamed me. She'd shown true grit, while I'd shown only weakness and hesitation. She'd acted, while I'd made excuses.

What would have happened if I'd acted that day, and insisted on helping the girl? Would the men have become violent? Were they carrying weapons? Could I have scared them off, or delayed them long enough to attract the attention of other drivers? Was there a chance that I could have saved that girl?

I'll never know what might have happened if I'd done things differently. We can't see down the paths we don't take: all we know are the paths we've taken. All I know is that I did nothing, and those men escaped with their prize.

Since that afternoon in northern Thailand, the path I've taken has been a highly unusual one, and it has led me to some extraordinary places. That was my first, fleeting glimpse into the world of human trafficking. It was soon to enter my life in a much more personal way, on a scale I'd never imagined – and this time, it came to stay.

ON THE ROAD TO FIND OUT

People travel for many different reasons. Some travel for the climate, the culture, or the exotic landscapes. Some travel for adventure and discovery, others for pleasure and relaxation. Some people travel simply to get away.

Born and raised in Australia, I'd been fortunate to have travelled more than most people. By April 2010, when I first arrived in Vietnam, I'd spent a total of four years abroad, and had lived in three foreign countries. Travel was one of my great loves, but I didn't see it as an end in itself. For me, travel was a form of education – it was my way of understanding the world and my own place in it.

Of all the places I'd travelled, Southeast Asia – with its wealth of history, culture, and religion, its extremes of poverty and overpopulation – had taught me the most.

By Australian standards, my family was quite ordinary – we weren't wealthy, or particularly privileged. Yet in Asia I saw how incredibly fortunate I was. The lifestyle I'd taken for granted in Australia was an impossible dream for billions of people here in Asia. I felt as though I'd received a winning ticket in the lottery of birth.

As with any form of education, I knew my travels would have to end – and, at the age of twenty-eight, I felt that time was rapidly approaching. My friends at home had long since finished their studies and were advancing in their careers. After a time, travel demands a meaning, a higher purpose. It was time to take the things I'd learned and apply them in some practical way.

It had been nineteen months since I'd packed up all my belongings and left a full-time filmmaking job in Australia. I'd been living and travelling in Southeast Asia ever since.

I didn't want to simply come to Asia, take my pictures, and return home unaffected. I wanted to make a difference in the world, a change for the better. I wanted to use the good fortune I'd been born with, together with my rapidly-accumulating knowledge and experience, to assist those who had been born into more difficult situations than my own – but how?

What could one person possibly hope to achieve on such a chaotic continent with so many complex and deeply-rooted issues?

As the months rolled by, and I travelled from one place to the next, I didn't feel I was getting any closer to answering that question. In fact, I felt as though I was only getting further away. The more I learned, the more complex the issues seemed to be, and the more frustrated I became with my own lack of action.

I was an adult, and it was time for me to start taking responsibility. This was my world now, as much as anyone's – and, with so much injustice and inequality, it simply wasn't the kind of world I wanted to live in.

Vietnam was the only country in Southeast Asia that held no particular appeal for me. I went there only because I'd reached the Cambodian border, and Vietnam lay right there in front of me. I'd come down with an especially nasty fever in Phnom Penh, and it trailed me for weeks as I moved slowly northwards along the Vietnamese coast. I was ill and exhausted, didn't really want to be there, and didn't know where I was going next.

I missed the sense of having a home, of being close to family and friends – but I wasn't ready to go back to Australia yet. Though I couldn't understand what it was, I felt as though I still had some purpose there in Asia. Until I could discover that purpose, I was simply going through the motions, checking off one "must-see" destination after another: Hoi An, Hue, Hanoi, Halong Bay...

One morning, I walked into a colourful little hostel by the beach. The moment I stepped through the door, I knew I'd found my direction again: it hit me in an instant. Against the back wall was a motley collection of abandoned books. One in particular caught my eye, and held it. It was a dark blue book with a single word printed large along the spine: "Tibet".

China itself interested me no more than Vietnam – but Tibet was another world, a strange and mystical culture nestled amongst the highest mountains on Earth, torn between ancient traditions and a stormy modern history. That's where I'd go.

I swapped the book for one of my own, and began to read. The more I learned, the more certain I became. In my mind, I'd already left Vietnam far behind.

In Hanoi, I applied for my Chinese visa. While I was waiting, I began to hear stories of Sapa, a remote market town in the northern mountains of Vietnam.

Sapa wasn't like the rest of Vietnam, I was told – in fact, it was hardly Vietnamese at all. It was populated mainly by hill tribes, each with their own colourful and distinctive traditional costumes, who came to town from remote mountain villages. I saw pictures of the spectacular rice terraces hewn like countless steps from the walls of vast hidden valleys.

Why not? I thought. I still had a few days left on my visa, and no intention of ever returning to Vietnam. It was now or never. Sapa was very close to the Chinese border – it was just a minor detour, and fit easily into my plans.

I had no way of knowing, of course, how Sapa would change all of my plans. In Sapa, I met not one but three people who would change my life completely, and lead me down paths I'd never imagined: Toan, May, and Dominique.

MISTY MOUNTAIN HOP

As the crow flies, Sapa is barely 250 kilometres from Hanoi – yet it took ten hours by bus to reach it.

I caught an overnight bus, and fought to sleep as it wove around corners and rattled along the broken road.

Once free of the sprawling capital, the highway followed the Red River northwest to the Chinese border. Here, two dusty cities faced each other across a muddy stretch of water: Lao Cai in Vietnam, and Hekou in China.

Our bus turned left at Lao Cai. The air became cooler and cleaner as the twin cities fell away behind us and the road snaked its way up into the mist that clung to the mountains. As dawn crept over us, I had the sense of entering some lost world, hidden away in some long-forgotten place.

The spell was broken on arrival in Sapa. A horde of

women and girls in dark tribal clothing swarmed the entrance to the bus. Bleary and half-asleep, I stumbled straight into their clutches. Hands stained green and purple thrust brightly-coloured handicrafts towards me.

"Hello!"

"Where you from?"

"You go trekking today?"

"Shopping? You buy from me?"

"Looking! Very cheap for you!"

"Maybe later? You promise?"

This was my first encounter with the Black Hmong people, who were soon to become such a major part of my life. They wore traditional costumes of the deepest blue, with elaborate bands of red, green, and white embroidered around the upper arms and waist. Many had coloured scarves tied about their heads, while white plastic slippers gave their feet little protection against the early-morning chill. Loops of tarnished silver jangled at their wrists and necks, and hung heavy from their earlobes.

Sapa, as I soon learned, was overrun with such girls and women, who spent their days plaguing the tourists on the streets. They hoped to make a little extra money for their desperately-poor families who otherwise lived by subsistence farming.

I fought my way through the throng and collected my backpack from the luggage compartment.

The bus had stopped by a lake. A heavy fog lay over us, and I didn't know where we were, so I simply followed the road. It led me to a small, rocky park where a palm tree nodded its head in the mist, alongside trees more appropriate to an alpine climate.

Beyond the park, I came to a large open space with a narrow, white-brick church on my left, and a broad set of stairs descending to Sapa's main square below me. An eight-pointed concrete star lay at the centre of the grassy square, surrounded by a ramshackle array of umbrellas and blue tarpaulins.

Here, local tribespeople had set up stalls selling cloth and clothing for tourists. I saw the same embroidered hats, bags, and purses the Hmong girls had thrust towards me outside the bus. Some of the items were meticulously handcrafted; others looked like cheap Chinese imports, in bright, tacky colours. I saw gourds, drums, and buffalo skulls with long, tapered horns.

Many of the locals were dressed in Black Hmong costumes; others wore Western-style clothing. Some of the women seemed to have their heads shaved beneath bright red headcloths. These, I later learned, were Red Dao people – Sapa's second-largest tribal group after the Black Hmong.

The square wasn't really square, and few of the streets seemed to meet at right angles. Sinuous roads snaked along the ridgelines and plunged towards the valleys.

As I emerged on the opposite side of the square, I found myself on Cau May Street, one of the principal streets of Sapa. Four short, dark men emerged from the mist, their pants rolled above their knees. Two carried a dirty grey sling suspended from a thick length of bamboo, the cloth distorted by the shape of a body inside. I saw a small, wrinkled hand emerging from the top of the sling, gripping the fabric, and realised that the men must be on their way to Sapa's hospital from one of the surrounding villages.

This was their village ambulance, and a sign that I'd entered a world very different to my own. I wondered how many hours they'd been walking already, in their cheap plastic sandals.

A short distance down Cau May Street, a set of rough stone steps turned aside and plunged through a gap between two buildings. The steps were overshadowed by tarpaulins, and crowded with women selling fresh produce and fried snacks. Locals shuffled up and down the stairs with large woven baskets on their backs.

I descended into a dim, cavernous space within a forest of towering concrete pillars.

Lines of rough wooden tables presented grim displays of dogs' heads and buffalo haunches. Enormous pigs lay strapped across motorbike seats, leaving little space for the riders. Chicken pieces sizzled over hot coals: not breasts or thighs, but bony heads and feet, with beaks and claws still attached.

Long white tables were lined with Hmong and Dao people slurping from bowls of soup. Many wore thin, ragged clothing, and looked as if they'd come directly from muddy fields.

I later discovered that the same tired-but-cheerful

women could be found cooking here seven days a week, every month of the year, from dawn until after dusk. They spent their lives ladling out simple but satisfying dishes of chicken and pork, rice and noodles.

The market I'd seen in the main square was the smiling face Sapa presented to tourists; this local market was Sapa's beating heart.

5:06AM: EVERY STRANGER'S EYES

A dollar bought me a bowl of steaming noodle soup, and a few more dollars bought me a room at a nearby guesthouse, where I showered and changed.

There was a small group of Americans and New Zealanders milling about the guesthouse lobby, preparing to hike down into the valley. They were to stay overnight in one of the tribal villages and return to Sapa the next day. I arranged to join them, and we set out a short time later.

Our guide was a young Hmong woman with a daypack and a folded umbrella. We descended from Sapa along steep, muddy tracks through scrub and sloping cornfields.

The morning fog, which had been drawn so tightly around us, began to melt away. It opened, lifted, and the world seemed to expand. The famed rice terraces gradually emerged on all sides, and hazy peaks crowded above.

Swaying stands of green bamboo erupted from the earth, their distant tips curling under their own weight, and clouds of orange butterflies rippled up from the trail at our approach.

Behind rough stone walls, we saw plantations of something we thought was marijuana, with its distinctive starred leaf. Our guide informed us it was in fact hemp, from which the traditional Hmong costumes were woven.

Stopping to pick a few leaves from a patch of low, bright-green plants growing by the side of the path, she told us to crush them in our hands. Our palms turned strangely greenish-purple.

There are five main groups of Hmong people in Vietnam, distinguished by the dominant colour of their clothing – the Black, White, Green, Red, and Flower Hmong (who wear multi-coloured costumes). This was the plant that gave the Black Hmong people both their name, and their appearance: it wasn't black at all, but indigo.

It was the Hmong women who would spin, weave, dye, stitch, and embroider the costumes. A single item of clothing could take months to produce, with the richly-embroidered sleeves and belts being the most demanding of all. The finished outfits were not only beautiful, but also practical and resilient – much like the women themselves.

Our small group descended to the valley floor, where a cloudy green river ran seething through the rocky shallows. After tottering across a long footbridge, we climbed high amongst the rice terraces on the far side of the valley.

We balanced along the narrow edges of the terraces, and followed rough dirt trails from one tiny cluster of homes to the next. We saw geese the colour of mud, chickens scratching in the dust, and fuzzy ducklings bumbling about with their wings tucked in at their sides.

Several of us took photographs of the children who greeted us by the side of the path, with their tangled hair and grimy faces. They were amused by our cameras, and even more so when we showed them the pictures we'd taken.

One of the Americans in our group was a professional photographer who toted a heavy bag of expensive lenses, and a camera that put mine to shame. From time to time, he would single out one of the local women to sit for a portrait. With his camera and a notebook, he took three things from his subjects before moving on: a photograph, a name, and a location.

"Xa – Y Linh Ho village," he'd jot in his notebook. Or, "Phong – Giang Ta Chai village".

His photographs were stunning, but there was a clinical detachment in his manner which made me a little uncomfortable. His work seemed to highlight the alien aspects of these women – their tribal clothing, their unfamiliar names, their exotic locations. I imagined his portraits exhibited in a gallery in America, each captioned with a foreign name and location – two snippets of information that said nothing about who the subject really was. Without any further context, these unfamiliar and often unpronounceable names would only widen the gap between the subject and the viewer.

The photographer struck me as a sort of butterfly collector, capturing these women and pinning them down, parading their curious patterns and colours before a voyeuristic audience.

I'd also been taking portraits of local people on my journey through Asia. I wasn't focused on strange landscapes, exotic costumes, or alien faces. Rather than stepping back to capture a scene, I'd get in as close as I could; in some cases, my camera lens was almost touching my subject's nose. I wasn't really photographing faces at all – what interested me most were people's eyes, and the emotions they held. I wanted to emphasise the things that we as human beings have in common, rather than those that set us apart.

It was a process that took more time and engagement. For a successful portrait, I had to overcome the language barrier and build a connection with my subject, however fleeting. I'd discard a technically-perfect photograph in favour of a blurred, hastily-composed shot – so long as it captured that human warmth and magic I was seeking.

I had an idle fantasy of exhibiting my portraits one day. As I watched the American photographer at work, and imagined him captioning his portraits with these alien names and locations, I decided I'd do just the opposite. Beneath every image in my exhibition, I'd place the same two words: "Human, Earth". Because no matter who you are, where you come from, which language you speak, or what the colour of your skin might be, we all have that much in common.

It was just a passing thought on my first morning in Sapa, and my imagined exhibition never became a reality, yet those two words – "Human, Earth" – were to echo through my life for years to come.

SURVIVING

In the depths of the valley, the land had been lush and green. Higher up, life seemed more desperate, stripped back to its most basic elements: a primal struggle for food and shelter.

From a distance, we'd seen clusters of people labouring across the face of the mountain. In a landscape of such vast dimensions, they'd seemed like insects gnawing gradually away at the dark green edges of the forest, exposing the raw earth of the terraces beneath. As we came closer, we saw their torn and dirty clothing, their faces streaked with sweat.

The rice terraces were filled with muddy, knee-deep water. They were broader down below, becoming steeper and narrower as they climbed the valley walls, before finally fading into the untamed forest above.

A buffalo with long curved horns and string tied

through its nostrils churned stubbornly along one of the muddy terraces. A stocky middle-aged woman followed behind, guiding the crude wooden plough it dragged. Her pants were rolled to the top of her thighs, her legs smeared with mud, her face expressionless.

Other women with colourful headscarves and babies strapped across their backs were digging and replanting rice in terraces nearby. Young children in grubby clothes worked beside them, and tiny girls gathered grass to feed the animals.

One man stood bent at the waist, hacking away at the thick brown clay of the mountainside: shaping another terrace, making space to grow another handful of rice. He seemed almost part of the earth himself, with a coat of wet clay drying over his skin and clothes.

Rice is one of the most labour-intensive crops on earth – a rice field is ten to twenty times more demanding than growing the same area of corn or wheat.

As I saw the endless lines of rice terraces receding into the hazy distance, I began to understand how truly daunting the work was. These terraces I'd seen as objects of beauty were something very different for the local people: they represented years of hard labour born of necessity. They were an endless struggle to build and maintain, to plant and harvest – and all for a few bags of rice.

The Hmong people, I learned, had come to Vietnam as refugees, fleeing war and persecution in China. They were a people without a country of their own, and were now scattered across southern China, Vietnam, Laos, and Thailand.

In Vietnam, finding the best land already taken, they had built their crude villages here in the rugged borderlands. Having previously lived in semi-nomadic communities at lower altitudes, the Hmong people had little expertise in building permanent settlements amongst the mountains.

At lower altitudes, farmers could grow two or even three rice harvests each year. Here, the people were able to harvest only once before the harsh winter returned, and it often wasn't enough to feed so many mouths. Many local families spent months of hunger surviving on whatever they could hunt or forage in the forests. There was a sense of everything just barely holding together, as the people here fought to maintain a tenuous toehold on life.

As a hazy afternoon glow filtered down through the bamboo and banana leaves, our little group arrived in a village which was to be our home for the evening. The buildings weren't huts exactly, but they weren't quite houses, either. They were ramshackle dwellings of bamboo and rough-hewn planks, which gave only the most basic shelter against the cold, rain, and occasional snow. They were cold, dark, damp, and smoky, with wide gaps in the walls. To cook meals, women squatted beside open fires in the middle of bare, uneven floors. The ventilation and sanitation were poor, and there was no running water. Few homes had toilets of any description, inside or out.

I'd been born in a country where our homes were miniature worlds unto themselves. We had glass windows, curtains, and an array of electric lighting options to make our homes as light or dark as we chose, at any time of day or night. We had heating, air-conditioning, and electric fans to control the temperature and air flow. We had refrigerators, stoves, and ovens to safely store and cook our food. We had sinks, baths, and showers, where we could summon forth streams, ponds, and waterfalls of crystal-clear, potable water in chemically-sanitised surroundings, at any temperature we liked. We had flushing toilets to eliminate our waste in comfort and privacy. We could control all of these things with the touch of a button, the flick of a switch, the twist of a handle.

I'd never had to worry about tending the plants and animals that produced my food, about hunting or foraging in the wild. In Australia we had supermarkets stocked with every conceivable kind of foodstuff shipped in from every corner of the world, regardless of the season. I could choose exactly what, how, and when I wanted to eat. The possibilities were limitless.

I bought my clothing ready-made, in whichever colours or styles I chose. I had so many different shirts, pants, and shoes at home that, on any given day, I could mix and match a new combination to suit my mood. I'd never met the people who'd made my clothes, nor seen the plants from which the fabric was made. I gave no thought to the time and effort it took to produce my clothing: I didn't have to.

Everything in my life was abstracted, disconnected. In Australia, I'd worked as a documentary filmmaker – work which had nothing to do with producing food, clothing, or shelter. Every day I relied on machines I could never hope to build or repair with my own hands. Illness, insanity, old age, and death had been kept at a comfortable distance from me.

My most valuable possessions were nonsensical strings of numbers, letters, and symbols, which gave me access to digital reservoirs of symbolic money. My bank transferred this "money" through convoluted channels to distant regions of the globe, investing it in ways I didn't understand, earning profits from the labour of people I'd never meet. When I needed money, I'd simply swipe a card and it would appear, as if by magic. I could swap it for anything I needed.

In Australia, we were among the most fortunate people to ever set foot on the planet. These people – the Hmong people – were among those left behind.

In Sapa, things I'd taken for granted simply didn't exist. Here, there was no insurance, and no assurances – life was something you paid for directly, each and every day, by the sweat of your brow. Here, a man's most valuable possessions were his buffaloes, his motorbike, his children, and the home he'd built with his own hands. All of these things could be snatched away by a rainy-season landslide in the blink of an eye.

The people here were barely surviving – and many, I learned, did not. I met a woman who had given birth to two dozen children, and lost eight in their infancy. In winter, icy winds blew straight through the houses, and children walked barefoot in the snow.

Seeing the raw fundamentals of life exposed, with all comfort and decoration stripped away, gave me a better sense of what life truly meant. Here, there was a proximity to death that highlighted the transience of life, giving it a more tangible value, making it more precious somehow.

The people here lived and died, and left little or nothing to show they'd ever existed. They produced no books, no monuments, no great works of art. Few could read or write, or even had birth certificates. Their highest art form was the clothing they wore until it fell apart.

I'd seen similar things in other parts of Southeast Asia – but what made Sapa truly remarkable was that so many of the local women and girls spoke English, and smatterings of other foreign languages.

As the least-valued members of their families, girls were sent out to peddle handicrafts to tourists. They had gradually learned to communicate directly with foreigners like me – not fluently, but well enough to bridge the vast divide between our two worlds. That simple connection made an incredible difference, for locals and travellers alike.

Long since marginalised geographically, politically,

and economically, this forgotten minority group in the far-flung mountains of northern Vietnam now had a line of communication with the outside world. Their endless rice terraces, built of poverty and desperation, were now bringing tourists, and the tourists were bringing far more than just money.

A QUESTION MARK

I stayed in Sapa for three more days, exploring the region by foot and rented motorbike. I rode through the mountains to remote villages where the locals seemed amazed to see a foreign face at all. It was true that Sapa was very different to anywhere else I'd been in Vietnam – or in the world, for that matter.

On my last evening in town, I lingered by Sapa's main square, reluctant to say goodbye. I would be leaving for China the next day, with no intention of ever returning.

One of Vietnam's true delights is *bia hoi* – literally, "draught beer". Every evening, opposite Sapa's main square, a local woman would set up a silver keg by the side of the road. On the pavement around it, she'd arrange a number of child-sized plastic tables and chairs. For 5,000 dong (about 25 cents), you could buy a large glass of very drinkable beer. On a warm Vietnamese evening, there is nothing better than to sit by the side of the road with a cold *bia hoi*, watching the world go by.

I sat down for one last *bia hoi* before leaving Vietnam. The Hmong girls were hawking their handicrafts on the street, and a circle of teenagers kicked a feathered shuttlecock between them in the square.

My thoughts turned again to Tibet – with the northern summer just beginning, it was the perfect time to visit the Himalayas. I was excited to reach Lhasa, the Tibetan capital, with its monumental palace and ancient monasteries hidden away on the roof of the world.

I finished my glass, paid, and turned to leave.

There was a group of young Vietnamese men sharing a jug of beer at the next table. One was a small man with short spiked hair, narrow black eyes, and a loose grin exposing crooked teeth. He spoke English, introduced himself as Toan, and told me to join his group for a beer.

Toan was Kinh – by far the largest and most powerful ethnic group in Vietnam, comparable to the Han in China. Although they were a minority in Sapa, the Kinh owned almost every hotel, restaurant, and shop in town. The Hmong people I'd met chose not to identify as Vietnamese – for them, the term was synonymous with the Kinh, whom they disliked and distrusted.

At that time, I didn't have a very high opinion of the Kinh people, either. Unlike many travellers who arrived on brief vacations, I'd been in Southeast Asia long enough to have some understanding of the local economy. As a foreigner, I was regularly quoted laughably-inflated prices, and expected nothing different. But while haggling could be a mutually respectful and enjoyable interaction with other people, many of the Kinh I'd encountered had a hard-nosed, take-it-or-leave-it attitude, which left me feeling cheated at every turn.

Toan was watching me, from beneath heavy-lidded eyes. He was insistent – too insistent – that I join his group, and his friends were waiting for my response.

Toan was impossible to read: no matter which emotion shifted across his face, nothing seemed to reach his eyes. Those eyes reminded me of every taxi driver and salesperson who'd cheated me in Vietnam.

It was a well-known con across Southeast Asia, luring a traveller into a night of revelry which ended with an exorbitant bill and the threat of violence. As a lone white male, I was an ideal target.

Two weeks earlier, in central Vietnam, I'd had an unpleasant experience with a group of six or seven young Kinh men who had invited me to eat with them. A few of them had spoken English and, as a traveller, I'd welcomed the opportunity to socialise with locals.

While they'd initially seemed very friendly towards me, after a time the young men seemed to forget I was there, and showed no further interest in speaking to me. I wasn't a naturally suspicious person, and hadn't understood what was happening until it was already too late.

After enjoying a large meal and numerous drinks, the young men had all stood up together, turned their backs on me, and simply walked out. The restaurant owner had clearly been aware of their little game, and turned to me expectantly.

I paid their bill and, while it hadn't been particularly expensive by Australian standards, the experience had left me feeling disgusted. They hadn't seen me as a human being, merely a wallet to be plundered. I'd been travelling to learn about foreign cultures, but that experience had taught me more than I'd wanted to know about Vietnam, and it wasn't a lesson I cared to repeat.

Toan told me again to sit down with his friends. The prudent thing to do was to walk away – but I didn't want to leave Vietnam with my prejudice and small-minded suspicions, so I decided to give him a chance. Perhaps he'd confirm my earlier experience, and perhaps he'd cancel it out.

I joined Toan and his friends for a beer. One beer became many, then Vodka Hanoi, then a midnight snack of pig's brains, and some hazy memories of stumbling back to my guesthouse several hours later.

The conversation had drifted between English and Vietnamese. At one point, Toan had asked me how I liked Sapa. I told him I loved it. He asked me if I wanted to live there, and said he could arrange a job for me, teaching English to the staff at his aunt's hotel and restaurant.

"Come and see me tomorrow at the Yellow Dragon," he said.

I awoke the next morning with my wallet intact, and

remembered Toan's offer. I did love Sapa, and would have loved to stay longer – but I had my doubts about Toan. Was he trustworthy? Was it a genuine offer, or just drunk talk?

I found Toan at the Yellow Dragon, and he showed me around. It was a deceptively large building, and seemed almost deserted. The hotel and restaurant were closed for renovations, Toan said.

The restaurant fronted onto a narrow laneway. Above and behind it were a cluster of large rooms on three levels. It wasn't a particularly fancy place, but looked comfortable enough.

Toan promised me my own room, and three meals a day. I'd have to teach only three hours a day, six days a week.

I was dubious – it seemed too good to be true. What was the catch? Why me, and not one of the countless other travellers that passed through Sapa every week?

Toan wasn't particularly interested if I had any relevant qualifications or experience. He didn't really seem to care about what exactly I'd be teaching, or how I might teach it. I wasn't sure it was a real job at all – it seemed like Toan had made the whole thing up on the spot.

If I was going to accept his offer, I'd first have to go back to Hanoi to extend my visa. Toan told me it would cost around 260 American dollars for a three-month extension – no small sum for a backpacker like myself. The same money would cover ten days' travelling, maybe more. It was quite a gamble on someone I'd barely met, and really didn't know at all.

The Yellow Dragon crouched at the edge of Sapa, on the very shoulder of the mountain. Like many hotels in Southeast Asia, it seemed a perpetual work-in-progress. Toan led me to the roof terrace where clumps of rusted steel rods sprang up from the bare concrete, awaiting the addition of another level.

From where we stood, the valley wall plummeted past trees and a few small houses into a vast green bowl below. The smooth brown curves of countless rice terraces were carved into the lower furrowed reaches of the valley. Beyond them, the forest grew thick and wild as the land rose steeply to a series of high, serrated peaks.

Toan pointed out the highest peak of them all, its mighty crown wreathed in clouds, looming directly across the valley.

"Fansipan," he said. The highest mountain in Vietnam.

It would be a magnificent panorama to wake up to: Tibet could wait a little longer. I shook Toan's hand, and told him I'd be back from Hanoi as soon as I could.

DAYS LIKE THIS

The three months I spent in Sapa were some of the best of my life.

I was given a large, freshly-renovated room at the Yellow Dragon, which served as both my classroom and private quarters. Toan and I propped up a whiteboard on the windowsill, with a half-circle of wooden chairs ranged around it.

I had ten students, mostly Kinh – Toan and two of his friends, plus seven waitresses, chambermaids, and kitchenhands. I taught basic grammar and vocabulary, and we had simple conversations. I tried to make the lessons relevant to work at the Yellow Dragon – I'd point out objects in the hotel room, or pretend to order from the menu. Those who spoke a little English helped those who had none.

One of my students, and the best by far, was a young

woman named Huong. She herself was an English teacher, having taught children in her own village. Her grammar and vocabulary were remarkable. As she'd never before had a native English-speaking teacher, however, Huong's spoken English was incomprehensible.

The Vietnamese language uses a complex tonal variation of the Latin alphabet, introduced by the French, and the pronunciation of the letters is often wildly different to ours. "D", "gi" and "r", for example, all sound like "z", making a phrase like "the rigid dirigible" particularly challenging for a Vietnamese speaker.

I could rarely grasp anything Huong said and, as two English teachers who couldn't speak together in that language, it was a continual source of embarrassment for both of us. I'd ask Huong to repeat herself. Finally, I'd ask her to write down what she wanted to say – and she would, in textbook English.

Toan was just the opposite. He'd never studied English, but had picked it up from tourists, having spent several years working as a tour guide. His spelling and grammar were atrocious, but he and I could stay up chatting late into the night, and often did.

Toan was crazy about Huong, and made no secret of the fact. I soon realised that Huong was the true reason I'd been invited to live in Sapa. As part of his relentless courtship, Toan had offered Huong something she'd never had: a native English-speaking teacher.

If Toan had hired me to impress Huong, his plan had failed utterly. Huong didn't reciprocate Toan's affection, and seemed to loathe me. Being so far ahead of the rest of the class, she was constantly frustrated with my repetition of the basics, and seemed to think I was making fun of her every time I asked her to write something down. My inability to understand her spoken English caused her to lose face with the class, an intolerable insult.

With our combined knowledge of English and Vietnamese, Huong and I could have been a formidable team in the classroom. Instead, we seemed to become adversaries.

I often caught Huong glaring at me, her face stony and impassive. I thought of her as cold and stubborn, and simply couldn't fathom Toan's obsession with her. Now, having come to better understand Huong and the world she was raised in, the only word I can find to describe her is "strong", and I say it with the deepest respect and admiration.

So long as she was set against him, Huong's strength of mind gave Toan no chance of wearing down her defences, and his dreams of marriage were doomed.

Toan had long since left his work as a tour guide to become a chef. He and the kitchenhands prepared the meals, which we all took together with Toan's aunt in the kitchen downstairs. Each meal saw a full table laid out with meats, tofu, spring rolls, a variety of vegetables and broths, roasted peanuts, and, of course, the ubiquitous steamed rice. In that kitchen I enjoyed some of the most amazing meals I'd eaten in Vietnam, and there was a wonderfully close-knit family atmosphere around the table.

One of Toan's favourite pastimes was presenting me with exotic Vietnamese dishes, to test my culinary courage. In a single memorable evening, we consumed stomach, liver, large and small intestines, fried chicken's feet, and a bowl of glaring red congealed blood. We washed it all down with a special kind of rice wine, which was filled with chunks of honeycomb and dead bees that would stick in your throat. At other times we ate dog, snake, buffalo, and tiny newborn chickens, skewered and barbecued. We ate bladder, brains, and boiled eggs with foetuses already formed inside.

The very thought of eating these things was repulsive, if not horrendous, and the textures were alien to me – but most of them tasted surprisingly good. Some were delicious, and became a regular part of my Vietnamese diet. They were a reminder that what we consider acceptable is really just a matter of cultural perspective, which varies wildly from one place to another.

When I wasn't teaching, I spent my days exploring Sapa and its surrounding villages, and getting to know the locals. The town was a tiny world unto itself, far from the world I'd left behind. It sat perched in the sky, inhaling and exhaling the clouds through its tangle of narrow streets and laneways.

Sapa was ever-changing, and seasons could pass hourly. Every day, I walked the same streets, and they were always new. They sparkled in the rain, burned beneath the sun, and vanished altogether in the mist.

Without warning, clouds would descend from crystal-clear skies and come tumbling through the streets. The world would be swallowed by a swirl of grey, for an hour or a day – then, just as suddenly, the curtain of fog could be torn aside to reveal endless blue skies beyond.

The blue skies drew the tourists into the streets, and the tourists drew the Hmong girls.

Like the act of breathing, there was constant movement, but it followed the same simple patterns. The tourists came and went in the buses and minivans, and seemed interchangeable from one another. The Hmong girls chased them up and down the streets, with the same handicrafts and the same old lines. Within these cycles of endless change was a very comforting and unchanging familiarity which, as a traveller, I'd rarely known: it felt like home.

ONLY A WOMAN

I can't say how or when I first met May and her friends. It seemed as if they'd always been there, sitting on the corner of the street.

The streets of Sapa swarmed with Hmong girls and women. There were girls as young as four or five years old with younger siblings strapped to their backs, brandishing gaudy trinkets. As they grew, they picked up smatterings of English and other foreign languages from their interactions with tourists. By the time they were teenagers, they spoke English remarkably well – in their own distinctive, endearing way – and could offer guided treks to their villages.

At first, I'd seen the girls as a nuisance. It was impossible to sit quietly without being pestered, even inside the cafés and restaurants, which made me doubly glad to take my meals at the Yellow Dragon. I often wore my headphones in the streets, to avoid being drawn into the Hmong girls' persistent sales banter.

As I began to understand how truly desperate life was in the Hmong villages, however, I started to see the girls in a different light. They had none of the advantages and privileges I'd taken for granted at home. Even amongst the Hmong people, I realised, the girls and women had the most difficult lives of all.

When I looked at my own options, the possible paths of my life seemed almost infinite, branching out in all directions across the globe – but for a Vietnamese Hmong woman, the possible paths of her life were typically few and miserable, leading through poverty, neglect, and abuse to an early grave.

A woman had very little say in her own future. Traditionally, she was given little choice even in the man she would marry, and had no reproductive rights.

As she didn't normally inherit any property, a woman spent her whole life tethered to a series of land-owning males – her father, husband, and sons – which could easily leave her in a precarious position. The local communities were rife with alcohol abuse, domestic violence, and a general disregard for women.

A woman's day typically began before dawn, and her life was one of hard, ceaseless labour. She took care of the home and family, raising her often very numerous children, weaving and embroidering clothing for them all, and toiling in the rice paddies. More often than not, her home was crumbling, her family was large, poor, and undernourished, and her resources were few.

I later learned of a woman in May's village who had been born perfectly normal in every way – but mute. Following the death of her parents, the family property passed to a brother who treated her badly and ultimately threw her out of their home. With nowhere else to go, she slept in rice paddies. At night, men would find her, and force themselves upon her. As a mute, she had no way of speaking out against them – and, once she had been defiled, she was considered unmarriageable. The woman gave birth to her first baby alone in a field. Surviving on the meagre charity of the local community and the occasional tourist who took pity on her, the woman came to live on a rough "bed" under a plastic sheet on the edge of a rice paddy, with very little protection from the stifling heat in summer, the freezing cold in winter, the crawling insects, and the men who intruded upon her whenever they chose.

That became her life, caring as best she could for her growing brood of fatherless children, perpetual reminders of the rape and abuse she had suffered. Even her children – with whom she was never able to speak – grew to despise her, referring to her not as "mother", but "that stupid woman".

That woman was my own age – we'd been born into the same world, at the same time. It was by no virtue of mine that I'd been born into a supportive family in a developed nation, just as that woman's misfortunes were no fault of her own. Her life could just as easily have been mine.

With the arrival of tourists in Sapa, new possibilities were emerging for the local Hmong women. Now, for the first time, the women had a chance to generate an independent source of income, far higher than anything else they might have earned.

For the local girls and women, picking up foreign languages and endearing themselves to tourists with their jests and jokes was no mere game: it was a means of survival. But the potential was far greater than that – it could also be a means of escape, of independence from the system that had trapped them for so long.

The Hmong women made sales, and received tips. Sometimes they benefited in other ways, too, with opportunities for education, travel, and even marriage to foreign men. Those who glimpsed life beyond their village rarely wished to return.

When the girls on the street saw me regularly and realised I was living in Sapa, they began to see me differently, too. They no longer tried to sell me their treks and trinkets, and their natural curiosity emerged. They wanted to know who I was, and what I was doing there in Sapa.

At the end of the lane, just a few steps from the Yellow Dragon, a dogleg in Cau May Street formed a small square with a hotel on one side and an Italian restaurant on the other. Both buildings had sheltered steps, and there was one particular group of girls who would often sit on the steps of one building or the other.

Initially, many of the girls had seemed quite similar: they wore the same traditional clothing, carried the same handicrafts, used the same sales pitches, and the sheer number of them had at first made it difficult to tell them apart. Many of their names, too, were confusingly similar. Before long, however, they began to distinguish themselves by force of their personalities, and I became friends with some of them.

There was Zao, who was small, thin, and sharp as a tack. Like most of the girls, Zao had been raised in poverty and had little or no formal education, but she was highly perceptive, and amazed me with her raw intelligence and wicked sense of humour. Zao always seemed two steps ahead. When she laughed, there was a glimmer in her eye that suggested there was something more to the joke, something she couldn't tell you because you'd never understand.

Pang was a portly, moon-faced girl, one of the loudest and most temperamental of the group. With her quick grin and flippant, dismissive attitude towards the world in general, Pang was a natural comedienne – but she had an emotional volatility which kept our friendship on a superficial level. In the space of a single conversation, Pang's mood could shift rapidly from raucous to sullen and back again, and she seemed to be forever holding her true feelings at arm's length.

Vu was a year younger than the other girls, and behaved like the runt of the litter. There was something disdainful in her attitude, as though she kept to the fringes of the group by choice, yet she always seemed to be watching slyly for an opportunity to take her share. Behind her cold detachment, I sensed a childhood of neglect and rejection – but Vu had a lighter side, too, and a radiant smile which shone out when she felt safe and comfortable.

There were two girls named Chu – Chu was one of the tallest girls, and Little Chu was the smallest. As one of the few who'd continued her education into high school, Chu was often absent from the group. When she was present, she often remained in the background: a quietly reserved girl, with a sweet, serious nature.

Little Chu, on the other hand, was a tiny little thing with an explosive laugh. Little Chu's family was among those that had abandoned traditional animistic beliefs in favour of Christianity.

The undeniable centre of attention, though, was May herself, with her mischievous grin, endless charisma, and irrepressible sense of humour. May was an extremely common name amongst Hmong women, and there must have been dozens of Mays on the streets of Sapa – but there were none quite like this one. May was brash, bold, and fearless – a little girl with a big smile, a big mouth, and a big heart.

I had no illusions about the Hmong girls. May and her friends had grown up on the streets, and had learned quickly how to pull heart strings for cash. They chased tourists through the streets and marketplace, endearing themselves with endless banter, and grinding down resistance with relentless tenacity.

I knew that the girls could be tricky and manipulative at times: they had to be. They'd learned to present a playful facade to tourists, hiding the harsh realities of their private lives. Sometimes the facade cracked, with a sudden flare of temper over a lost customer or a seemingly insignificant sum of money. It was a sharp reminder that, although we walked the same streets, the girls and I lived in two very different worlds.

But May was different from the others. While some girls seemed to be constantly scanning for opportunities and calculating their odds, May threw herself into life fearlessly, selflessly. The jokes and laughter came more naturally to her, and she seemed to genuinely enjoy her time with tourists.

May's personality was so closely aligned with her work that she hardly seemed to be working at all. She seemed to receive the lion's share of attention and money from tourists with the least amount of effort. Other girls tried to emulate her, standing as obvious imitations in the shadow of the genuine article.

May's charisma and Zao's intelligence made them the natural leaders of the group. Their friendship stood at the group's core, and drew the other girls to it.

Once I came to recognise May and her friends, it seemed as though they were everywhere I went – on the streets, in the square, by the lake, at the markets. They became an ever-larger part of my life, and I began to look forward to meeting them each day, to the jokes and stories we shared.

The girls I'd once seen as a nuisance now appeared to me as something remarkable, and their lives took on an almost historical importance. With their new, independent source of income, May and her friends stood at the leading edge of a social revolution which was capable of turning their entire culture upside-down.

Would they be among the first generation of empowered women to break free from centuries of male domination, and take control of their own lives? Would they forge a new path, not only for themselves, but for all of the Hmong women in Sapa?

THE GIRL IN THE DIRTY SHIRT

May had been born and raised in a village several hours' walk from Sapa. She was the youngest of five children, with two brothers and two sisters. Like the vast majority of the Vietnamese Hmong, May's parents were subsistence farmers, growing rice, corn, and vegetables to feed the family. They kept buffaloes, pigs, ducks, and chickens at their home.

As a child, May was friendly, helpful, and well-liked. Zao, Pang, and Chu lived nearby, and they all played together when they were young.

May never went to school. Few of her friends received anything more than the most rudimentary education, if that. Most of the Vietnamese Hmong see little point in formal education.

Rural Vietnam is not a meritocracy, in which a job is given to the most suitable candidate. The best jobs are bought – at a price far beyond what subsistence farmers can afford, and often far beyond the wages of the job itself. A government position in the village, for example, would cost thousands of dollars; in Sapa itself, much more. Wealthy families purchased positions of power for their children, and the money paid was recovered by taking advantage of that power, thereby enforcing a system of institutionalised corruption.

With few resources and little political power, marginalised groups like the Hmong found themselves trapped inside a system that was stacked against them.

May was born at a time when Vietnam had recently opened to Western tourism. Intrigued by the colourful tribal groups, foreign tourists had begun trekking from Sapa to the villages, and were willing to pay good money for traditional clothing and jewelry.

Scrambling at the opportunity, local women began producing more handicrafts. Like most girls in the village, including both of her sisters, from a young age May began selling hats and bracelets to tourists.

At that time, the path from Sapa to May's village was a longer, more difficult trail, and there were no restaurants in the village. The trekking groups would carry their own food, often picnicking on the grass beside the river.

When May was small, she'd go there with her friends to sell handicrafts, and they'd pursue the trekking groups along the trail. With the money they earned, May and her sisters helped support their family. May's parents were able to build an extension to their home in solid wood, rather than bamboo. They were also able to afford extra food, clothing, pigs, chickens, and fertiliser for their crops.

By the time they were eleven or twelve years old, May and her friends were making the long trek to Sapa to sell handicrafts to tourists on the street there. At first, they would return to sleep in the village with their families each night; later, they began sleeping in town.

For 7,000 dong (about 35 cents) per night, a girl could sleep on the floor in a Kinh house, but the girls disliked these houses. As soon as they could afford to do so, May and her friends began sleeping together in a series of very basic rented rooms.

A typical room was a small space of bare concrete with a tiny, cold-water bathroom behind a partition, and only the most rudimentary furniture. Having lived all their lives in muddy huts, the girls didn't consider these rooms uncomfortable.

Here, away from their families, the girls became a tightly-knit family to each other. It was a chance for them to escape the restrictions of their highly traditional culture – but there were also dangers in growing up without the guidance and support of their parents.

When I met May and her friends, in mid-2010, they had been living in Sapa for about two years, and had only recently begun working as tour guides. May's elder sisters, Cho and Dinh, both sold handicrafts on the streets of Sapa. Cho had a housekeeping job at a nearby hotel, and joined May's group in her free time.

With her long freckled face and more serious nature, Cho stood in stark contrast to her smiling, round-faced sister. I never came to know her well, and never knew Dinh at all.

In total, there were ten girls in May's group. It was very rare to see them all together, with two or three girls attending school, Cho working shifts at the hotel, and various girls out trekking at any given time.

I struggled to understand the girls' names, ages, and familial relations. Certain things that are rigidly defined in the West can be very fluid amongst the Hmong, and surprisingly difficult to grasp.

In 2010, May and most of her friends claimed to be fourteen years old, by the Western count, which was plausible. However, most of the girls had never known their birthdates, and only guessed at the year. Many had been born at home to illiterate parents, with no birth certificates or calendars to mark the occasion.

When giving their ages, they often counted an extra pre-natal year – "one year in the stomach", as they put it. They invented birthdays for themselves, and changed them as they pleased.

May did have a birth certificate, claiming she was born in December 1995 – although if it was issued after the fact, it is likely inaccurate. At various times, May and her family have given her birth year as anywhere between 1990 and 1998.

The girls' names were also very changeable. Many of their given names had three different spellings in

Hmong, English, and Vietnamese. Adding to the confusion were many names that were identical or very similar, a very limited number of surnames, and a profusion of nicknames, so that the same girls were often known by different names to different people. Family names applied to larger clan groups, rather than nuclear families, and could be stated before or after given names.

May and many of her friends belonged to the same clan and shared the same family name. Some of the girls were sisters or cousins, and others claimed to be, though the terms were often used loosely. May and Zao were cousins.

May and her friends fascinated me, giving me a unique glimpse into a culture so alien to my own. Though only half my age, the girls had developed a remarkable strength and resilience, having survived hardships and deprivations I could scarcely imagine.

Though they'd had little formal education among them, the girls had been raised in a fierce, high-stakes environment. In some ways, they were incredibly street-smart – while in other ways, they were still very naïve, and we had much to learn from each other.

There were things that disturbed me about the Hmong girls, too.

In more developed countries, families are smaller, and children tend to be a conscious, controlled choice. They are wanted. The Vietnamese Hmong had children for very different reasons – to work the land, and to look after them in their old age. A child was a burden until it became useful to its parents, and boys were valued more highly than girls.

In Sapa, a lack of sexual education and contraceptive options made having children less of a conscious choice. Families were generally large, and infant mortality rates were extremely high. While so many births and deaths went unrecorded and concrete statistics were lacking, it seemed as many as a third of children died in their infancy.

Traditionally, a Hmong woman gave birth in a squatting position at home, in squalid conditions. Seeking medical assistance was perceived as a sign of weakness. Parents prepared nothing for a baby until after it had survived the birth, and the child was not given a name until it had survived its first week.

May and her friends had been raised with a sense of insignificance and inferiority, and had been surrounded by death from an early age. On the streets of Sapa, they spent long days in intense competition against even their closest friends. The result was an emotional coldness that was alien to me.

As a result of their poverty, many Hmong people in Sapa seemed unable to see beyond their next meal, leaving them extremely vulnerable to manipulation from the forward-planning Kinh, from tourists, and from each other.

The combination of their emotional detachment and disturbingly short-sighted attitudes led to a willingness amongst many of the Hmong girls to betray even those closest to them for the sake of a momentary advantage.

I was concerned for May and her friends. Countless new paths were opening up before them – but which would they choose? Even if they could escape the confines of their male-dominated culture, would they recognise their own power and grasp the possibilities that lay before them?

From their work with tourists, some of the young Hmong women in Sapa found themselves with more money than they'd ever imagined – only to squander it on cocktails and garish Chinese-made clothes, while their own families went hungry at home in the villages.

In the new world that lay before them, the greatest obstacle May and her friends faced was themselves – or so I believed. I hadn't yet glimpsed the true danger that lay in wait for them.

Within the next twenty months, no less than five of those ten girls were kidnapped in separate incidents. The other five were to become suspects in their disappearances – and I was to find myself in the middle.

SAY YES

After my first month in Sapa, I went back to Hanoi for a few days.

An overnight bus to Hanoi left Sapa every day at dusk, from the park by the lake, and that's where I met Dominique. Arriving uncharacteristically early, I found the bus almost empty. Dominique and her friend were sitting near the back.

Dominique was a French-Canadian who'd just spent a month in rural Laos as part of a college anthropology project. She'd decided to stay on in Asia, backpacking with a girlfriend for another two months. They'd come overland from Laos and had just spent a few days in Sapa, on their way to Hanoi.

Before we left Sapa, Dominique and I were already caught up in conversation. We spent the whole night chatting together in hushed tones while the rest of the bus slumbered around us.

As I gradually discovered, Dominique was gorgeous, charming, intelligent, funny, unattached, and interested. Beyond her more obvious characteristics, there was something magical about her, something more difficult to define. Friends often commented on my energy and enthusiasm for life, but I rarely saw the same qualities in others. Dominique was different: she was vibrant, alive in a way that few people are.

I was smitten – and Dominique felt the same way about me. We spent five days together in Hanoi, then she doubled back to visit me in Sapa for another five days.

When I was a teenager, I'd spent a lot of my time drawing. It took a lot of time, because I'd set unusually high standards for myself. Not only did I want the picture as a whole to be perfect, but I wanted every stroke and curve within the picture to be just right, too. Dominique was that kind of perfect, and every time I saw her smile, she reminded me how lucky I was.

When Dominique came back to Sapa, I introduced her to May and the Hmong girls. They spent their afternoons together while I taught my classes at the Yellow Dragon, and Dominique soon began referring to the girls as her "Hmong sisters".

Once again, Dominique left Sapa on the overnight bus, kissing me goodbye just metres from where we'd first met. Dominique was a once-in-a-lifetime kind of woman, I knew that. I asked her to come to Tibet with me, after she'd finished travelling with her friend. She said yes.

My parents had travelled through the Himalayas together before they were married. I wondered privately if Dominique and I would one day be telling the same story to our own children.

May and her friends insisted I was a bad boyfriend because I didn't cry when Dominique left. May told me she missed Dominique more than I did, which I found difficult to believe. She said her love for Dominique was bigger than a buffalo. I told her my love for Dominique was bigger than three buffaloes, with a few chickens thrown in for good measure. We haggled over buffaloes, chickens, pigs, and elephants, until finally May declared that her love for Dominique was bigger than the sky. That seemed like a hard act to follow, and I let her claim the victory – further proof, of course, that my feelings for Dominique weren't sincere enough.

Pang told me if she ever saw me talking to another woman, she'd murder me, then write to Dominique to tell her all about it.

I smiled, and told her there was no need.

REVOLUTION 1

I needed something to distract me from thinking about Dominique, and Toan had the perfect solution.

While I'd been in Hanoi, Toan had rented a small, horrifically ugly restaurant. It was a monument to mediocrity, painted a revolting shade of dark brown. Its name, written large across the front, was 'Vietnamese Restaurant' – hardly an imaginative name for a restaurant in Vietnam. It wasn't hard to see why it had failed.

Toan wanted to transform it into a bar and café for tourists, and asked me if I had any ideas for redecoration. As it happened, I did.

There were only a handful of countries around the world that still identified as Communist, and this was the first time I'd ever lived in one. I found myself oddly disappointed – I'd expected something more unusual. Apart from the occasional hammer-and-sickle on public buildings, propaganda banners strung up in the cities, and some blocky, warlike statues in Hanoi, I'd seen little to distinguish Vietnam as a Communist country.

In the absence of any real Communist curiosities, I proposed we create our own: an irreverent, over-the-top, uber-Communist café filled with wartime propaganda.

I wanted to call it 'Uncle Ho's'. Uncle Ho was the familiar yet respectful term the locals used for Ho Chi Minh, the leader of Vietnam's Communist revolution. To me, it was just a funny name for a bar. Uncle Ho, however, remains a near-sacred figure in northern Vietnam, and Toan was afraid we'd be arrested. I could do whatever I liked, he said, as long as I kept Uncle Ho out of it.

I called it 'Charlie's' instead, thinking of the US war films I'd seen, where "Charlie" was used as a slang term for a Communist fighter. Toan gave me brushes, paints, and a team of workers, and we painted the whole place, from floor to ceiling.

Bright red, of course.

In Hanoi, I'd visited some shops that sold prints of old propaganda posters from the American War (as it is known in Vietnam) and from the Cold War era, and I'd brought some back to Sapa with me. We copied images from the posters, painting them huge across the walls. The centrepiece was a giant mural of a Vietnamese soldier hefting a rocket launcher.

Toan loved the concept – in fact, he took it further than I did. He wanted to buy Vietnamese flags to use as tablecloths. Instead, we made an enormous one – a bright red flag with a huge yellow star in the centre – to suspend from the ceiling. Toan bought North Vietnamese army helmets which we used as lampshades, and tried to source some barbed wire for decoration. I'd found a star-shaped bookcase which we painted bright yellow, along with all the tables and chairs.

I had some amusing translations of patriotic slogans from the propaganda posters, and began painting them around the walls in blocky yellow letters: "THE SOLDIER IS VERY PROUD", "WHEN UNCLE HO SAYS VICTORY IT MEANT VICTORY", and "WE ARE AN INVINCIBLE".

Toan gave me five workers. Some he said were his brothers; I didn't know exactly what that meant, since he referred to me the same way. Health, safety, and hygiene left a lot to be desired amongst Toan's crew, to say nothing of their work ethic. They were overabundant and undermotivated: they'd come in late, start slowly, put in maybe an hour's work, get roaring drunk at lunchtime and then melt away upstairs to sleep it off.

The restaurant had come with a fully-stocked bar, and I suspect Toan's workers were being paid in alcohol, in which case they certainly made the most of the opportunity. It didn't help that none of them spoke a word of English, and I spoke no Vietnamese. I ended up doing most of the work myself, and did so happily.

We had a chronic shortage of turpentine and, with no way to wash off the paint, it went through everything. It was all over my clothes, camera, and netbook, and soon found its way onto my towels and bedding at the Yellow Dragon.

As if things weren't messy enough already, May and her friends would come around, pick up any abandoned brushes, and do their best to paint my arms and legs while I was working. It was summer, and I often painted shirtless. May, of course, decided to scrawl her name in large red letters across my torso. Without enough turpentine to wash it off properly, it stuck there for almost a week.

The days were fun, and the evenings were even better. After Toan and his friends finished work, they'd come around and we'd all paint together. When I wasn't painting, I was putting together a soundtrack of US war-era rock songs, from bands like The Doors and Creedence Clearwater Revival. I threw in soundbites from classic films: Robin Williams' "Goooooooooood morning, Vietnam!", Robert Duvall loving the smell of napalm in the morning, Forrest Gump explaining that Vietnam is a whole other country, that kind of thing.

We never had a grand opening Communist Party as intended: Charlie's opened almost by accident. We kept the front doors open for ventilation, and curious passers-by began wandering in off the street, as if it were an art gallery. If we happened to be eating or drinking, we'd invite them to join us and, before we quite realised what was happening, Charlie's was already in full swing.

Charlie's was an instant hit with locals and foreigners

alike. Vietnamese families came for the food, and travellers of all ages and nationalities came to drink. May and her friends loved it too, and brought in more customers.

Another café, a few doors down, saw our success and began painting their own murals. Toan's aunt asked me to redecorate the restaurant at the Yellow Dragon, despite it having barely reopened after their last renovation.

My Kinh, Hmong, and foreign friends all began gathering at Charlie's, and it immediately became my new home-within-a-home.

THE GOOD OLD DAYS

It was at Charlie's that I helped May and her friends set up their first email and Facebook accounts, so they could keep in contact with the tourists they met. We'd sit together at the tables outside the café, checking their messages and typing responses on my netbook.

I helped the Hmong girls move what little furniture they had between the tiny rooms they rented. If May saw me walking in the rain, she'd insist on lending me her umbrella – without knowing when I'd see her again, or if she might need it before then.

Other foreigners saw me at home in Sapa, and came to me for advice on the best place to arrange a trek, or what a reasonable price for handicrafts might be. I'd refer them on to May and her friends. In turn, May and her friends would bring customers to Charlie's.

Charlie's was booming. Wherever we went in Sapa,

Toan rarely let me pay for anything. He and his friends helped me in countless other ways, too – whether I was going to the doctor or the barber, or buying new clothing, they made it very easy for me, and made sure I paid the local prices.

Toan cooked a lavish lunchtime banquet at the Yellow Dragon. I took photographs of it and the restaurant, to help with promotion, and we ate it together with the staff.

I'd travelled through dozens of countries, interacting with local people in many different ways, but these relationships in Sapa were some of the most beautiful I'd ever known. We all made each other's lives better, easier, and far more enjoyable. Most remarkable of all, I'd unwittingly succeeded in bringing together friends from opposing sides of a deep ethnic divide.

The girls invited me to a Hmong wedding in the village, which was very different to any other wedding I'd seen. The main feature was an absurd quantity of "happy water", which isn't really water, but rice wine – which isn't really wine, but a rather potent spirit.

(Locals tell you that happy water won't get you drunk, just happy, though my Kinh friends and I had disproved this theory on more than one occasion.)

Though I'd arrived at the wedding quite early in the morning, the only ceremony I saw consisted of endless, unavoidable rounds of toasts, to everyone and everything in sight, each reinforced by a shot of happy water. We sat cross-legged on the floor of a local home, gorging ourselves on pork, rice, and vegetables, and putting the proverbial skunk to shame.

This wasn't just a special time in my life, I realised: it was a special time for all of us.

My Kinh friends – mostly male – were in their ascendency. Toan and his friends would grow and flourish, inheriting hotels and restaurants, becoming the ruling class of Sapa. They'd soon have wives, families, and greater responsibilities of their own.

May and her friends were on a very different path. Hmong girls in Sapa usually married in their teens – some as young as twelve or thirteen years old. Within a few short years, May and her friends would be expected to surrender the freedom they'd known in Sapa. They would soon be scattered amongst the outlying villages, bound to husbands and growing broods of children. They had only this fleeting moment to call their own.

My own path would inevitably lead me away from Sapa, and this special bond I shared with my Hmong and Kinh friends would also be gone. I'd never been back to any of the foreign countries I'd lived in, and I expected Vietnam would be no different. Even if I did return someday, I knew it could never be the same.

My time in Sapa was brief, but intense. My life there had become a sort of hurricane, a whirl of constant movement. I rode a motorbike through the mountains, exploring villages, caves, and waterfalls. I hiked out through the fields and forests, slept in huts, and swam in rivers. I ate fruit from the trees and grapes from the vine. My evenings were filled with drinking and dancing and singing with my friends. I was invited to dinner parties and celebrations. Foreign friends, and friends of friends, came to find me there, and Toan threw dinners for them at Charlie's.

At the centre of all the excitement was a calm and contentedness like none I'd ever known. I was living every day to its fullest potential, following it wherever it might lead me. I slept deeply, and spent mornings alone in quiet contemplation, watching the mist pour over the windowsill and roll into the room. I lay in the sun beside the river, and simply enjoyed being alive.

There was nothing more I could have asked for – except, of course, to see Dominique again.

NEVER UNDERSTOOD

Living with such vast gaps in language and culture, there were many things in Sapa I didn't understand.

In almost three months of jokes and laughter with May, there were occasional misunderstandings between us, and times I accidentally triggered her.

The greatest upset to our friendship came one day when I jokingly called May bossy. To show me how annoyed she was by my comment, she made a point of avoiding me, for several days.

When she finally reappeared, May began acting even more friendly than usual towards me. She'd begun to worry that she'd been treating me too harshly, and if she didn't smooth things over between us, she thought *I* was going to start getting upset with *her*.

The comical part was that I'd been utterly oblivious to the whole episode. I hadn't even noticed that May had been giving me the cold shoulder – the Hmong girls were often out trekking, and I was used to their absences.

I'd forgotten having called May bossy, and – until she explained it to me – I'd had no idea she'd been so upset by it. I apologised, promised never to do it again, and we both had a good laugh about our little misunderstanding.

Another time, when visiting one of the villages outside Sapa, I'd taken a funny photo of a buffalo licking its own nostril. I shared it on Facebook and, as a joke, tagged May as the buffalo.

When she saw the photo, May was almost in hysterics, and didn't seem to know whether to laugh or cry. While she saw the humour in it, the photo filled her with an inexplicable horror.

I was baffled. I'd never seen May have such a powerful emotional reaction to anything, and couldn't imagine why she would be so deeply affected by a picture of a buffalo.

May was still new to Facebook. She didn't understand its finer points, and wasn't familiar with the terminology. It took a long, confused, and emotionally-charged conversation before I understood why she was so upset.

To her mind, I'd created an unbreakable bond between her and the buffalo. It was as if I'd put a black mark on her permanent record, and forever tainted her social life. Wherever she went from that day forward, May would be the buffalo girl.

I showed May how quick and easy it was to remove her name tag from the photo. She was incredibly relieved to learn that she wasn't, in fact, cursed to live out the rest of her life shackled to a ridiculous photo of a buffalo.

Once they'd been explained to me, these misunderstandings with May made sense, and we could laugh about them afterwards.

With Pang, however, there was a regular flurry of little dramas which were never explained, and never made much sense to me. These misunderstandings kept a distance between us, and left us unable to build a more meaningful friendship.

The most serious misunderstanding I had during those three months in Sapa, though, was with Toan's aunt.

Toan's aunt was a thin, conservative woman who owned the Yellow Dragon, and lived there in a large suite on the top floor. At Toan's request, she'd allowed me to come and live at her hotel. We ate our meals together but shared no common language, and relied on Toan as a go-between.

Toan's aunt belonged to the older generation. When she was a child, her country had been at war with people who looked like me – yet she treated me very well. We liked each other, and were always on good terms.

After meals, Toan's aunt would often invite me to drink a glass of green tea with her in the restaurant. We'd spend long minutes sitting together in a warm and comfortable silence, like two old friends.

Then one day I found myself embroiled in a strange and sudden drama with Toan's aunt. It was made even stranger by the fact that there wasn't a single word spoken between us, and we barely even saw each other all day.

When the newly-renovated hotel and restaurant were reopened to the public, life became busier for all of us. Sometimes on weekends, when the hotel was fully booked, I was asked to vacate my room for a night or two and move to a small, dark room downstairs. It was an inconvenience, but never a problem.

One morning, soon after Dominique's departure, one of the hotel staff asked me to move downstairs. I packed up my belongings and shifted them into the spare room without question.

When I turned in my key, however, I realised it was still only a Thursday, and the hotel didn't seem particularly busy.

After making a few inquiries, I realised that Toan's aunt had no intention of ever moving me back upstairs – in fact, she seemed to be looking for a way to get rid of me altogether. She didn't want me living or working in the hotel anymore.

I wasn't due to leave Sapa for another six weeks, and could hardly believe what I was hearing. Literally overnight, I'd become a persona non grata at the Yellow Dragon, and couldn't imagine what had triggered such a sudden reversal.

After a long, strange day, Toan finally uncovered the reason behind his aunt's decision.

When Dominique had come to visit me in Sapa, she'd stayed with me at the hotel. Toan's aunt knew that Dominique and I were unmarried, and disapproved of us sharing a bed in her hotel. While she tolerated that kind of thing amongst her other guests, she felt it was inappropriate behaviour for a staff member.

Worse still, that bed was positioned directly above the shared staff quarters, where the unmarried teenage girls slept. Without our realising it, Dominique and I had been keeping the girls awake at night, and giving them the wrong sorts of ideas.

Small-town Vietnam still held quite traditional values. Toan's aunt had never married, and she and the girls at the Yellow Dragon presumably had no experience with sex. The last thing they needed was an unmarried, sexually-active foreign man among the staff.

To my mind, it was only natural that Dominique would stay with me, and I'd never imagined that her presence might cause any disruption. Toan's aunt, on the other hand, seemed to consider my behaviour a disgraceful betrayal of her trust, which put an end to any previous arrangements between us.

She'd cancelled all my classes, and didn't want to see me anymore.

Fortunately, Toan refused to let me go so easily. He petitioned his aunt with apologies and assurances until at last she relented. I was returned to my room, and resumed teaching the next day.

Toan's aunt took me back into her good graces, and

we resumed our tea-drinking sessions as if nothing had ever happened.

It was a confusing day, filled with events that seemed momentous at the time. It wasn't until much later that I realised there were other, far more important things happening in Sapa that I'd entirely failed to understand.

BLOOD BROTHERS

One evening towards the end of my time in Sapa, I was at Charlie's helping some of the Hmong girls read and write their emails. I knew I was missing dinner at the Yellow Dragon, but that was fine – the hotel staff were used to my occasional absences, and I could go out to eat something later.

This time, however, Toan sent a messenger to find me, insisting I join them for dinner. That had never happened before. I excused myself, and went back to the hotel.

Rather than eating downstairs in the kitchen as usual, the staff had closed the restaurant for the evening, and prepared a long banquet table in the centre of the room. I was the last to arrive.

Something had happened between Toan and Huong – I never asked what it was – but Huong had suddenly quit her job, and was leaving Sapa first thing the next morning. Toan was devastated.

Huong's family lived on the flatlands, halfway between Sapa and Hanoi. Toan couldn't bear to see Huong simply get on a bus and disappear, so he'd prepared a farewell dinner for her, and offered to drive her home the next day on his motorbike. He asked me to come with him, on a second bike.

It was a four or five hour ride on dangerous, winding roads each way. I was unlicenced and uninsured, but I wasn't going to refuse Toan, seeing the state he was in.

The three of us were up at sunrise. We rode down out of the clouds, and over the mountains towards the sea. I had no information, no map, and no idea where we were going. As it turned out, none of us did. Huong had only ever made the journey by bus, and didn't know the way.

After months in the mountains, the tropical lowland air felt like a hot, thick soup. The strap holding Huong's luggage to my bike snapped, and her bags were ready to fall off. Huong was travel-sick and looked like she was ready to fall off Toan's bike, too.

We broke off the main road and over another line of hills, through a provincial town, and out onto rough dirt roads to the middle of nowhere. Huong's extended family lived in a cluster of mud-walled, thatch-roofed buildings by a small pond, surrounded by a cluster of banana and cinnamon trees. The men were welding and painting boilers in the yard. The family greeted us with a late lunch served on a mat in the middle of the floor: unidentified parts of unidentified animals, washed down with beer and plenty of rice wine. None of them spoke any English, but they treated us wonderfully.

A storm drifted across in the evening, as the men sat smoking tobacco from a long bamboo waterpipe. Huong squeezed into one bed with her parents, leaving the second bed to Toan and me. The large shared bedroom was also the dining room and the family room, and was a bustle of activity from six o'clock the next morning.

The family loved having us there, and was full of curiosity about Australia – or *Uc*, as they call it in Vietnam. They urged us to stay another night, but Toan had to get back to work at the Yellow Dragon.

I'd never had a good connection with Huong – but in her home, with her family, I saw a different side to her. For the first time, I began to understand how difficult her life must have been, and found myself with a deep respect for her strength and courage. Huong had worked hard for what little she had. I could easily understand her resentment of me, the foreigner who'd come breezing into a wonderful life and an undemanding job in the middle of his holidays, while she fought every day for her family and future.

What was I, there in Vietnam? I was no longer a tourist – but I would never truly be a local, either. I felt caught between worlds.

After a breakfast of intestines, liver, and the inevitable rice wine, Toan and I were back out on the road. The open road and sunshine put me in an excellent mood. Toan, having left Huong behind, was utterly heartbroken.

The wonderful thing about a motorbike is that you can take whatever you happen to be feeling and convert it directly into kilometres per hour. Instead of riding back to Sapa, Toan and I just rode, letting the road lead us. The sunshine began to work its magic on Toan: after an hour or so spent riding in the opposite direction to Sapa, he was pumping his fist in the air and hollering to the world at large.

A few minutes later, the skies opened and the monsoonal rains fell as a solid grey mass upon us. They struck without warning, and with incredible force. I couldn't even see the sunglasses in front of my face, or the edge of the road to get off it. A black car with no headlights very nearly sideswiped us both. I saw Toan's tail-light flash red, and dived blindly off the shoulder after it. We holed up by the side of the road while the worst of the deluge passed.

We were back on the main highway now, and when the storm stopped, the trucks began: battalions of them, howling down from the Chinese border. The highway was a major trucking route connecting Hanoi and China – and yet it was just a narrow, potholed road with a single lane in each direction, twisting its way around the valley wall.

In Vietnam, road markings are purely decorative. Some people drive on the left, some drive on the right, and some come straight down the middle. Others can't seem to decide, and drift from one side to the other. On Vietnamese roads, size matters, and the only rule that counts is: big wins.

Stone-faced drivers brought their rigs hurtling around blind corners on the wrong side of the slick wet road. Screaming walls of solid steel, they were moving too fast to stay in their own lane, and were too big to argue with.

The carnage was everywhere. We saw a cement mixer by the side of the road with its cab torn almost completely off. Another truck had smashed itself to pieces as it rolled down a steep incline, before coming to a mangled rest in a grove of bananas trees far below.

Some fifteen thousand people are killed on Vietnamese roads every year, most of them motorcyclists. Three times in two hours I felt the hot breath of a truck's cab as it came hissing past me, far too close for comfort. Jamming on the horn and throwing out curses in their wake seemed like small revenge for such narrow escapes.

Over the past fifteen years, I've ridden motorbikes all over the world. That twisted and broken Vietnamese highway, gleaming wet and thrumming with trucks, remains the most hair-raising ride of them all.

It was dark by the time Toan and I arrived back in Sapa. I stumbled to my room, and fell into an exhausted sleep.

Every evening, local women would set up barbecues in the lane beside the church. The next day, Toan and I went there with our Kinh friends. It was a beautiful evening, with a clear sky above, and lightning strobing around the tops of the mountains.

When I'd first arrived in Sapa, most of the Kinh people there had viewed me the same way as any other tourist: a business opportunity, and nothing more. When I began living there and spending time with Toan's friends, I'd been something of a novelty – but as the months passed, I began to count Toan's friends amongst my own.

As Toan declared, often and loudly, I was no longer a foreigner there: "You are Vietnamese people!"

On this particular evening, in an unusually reflective mood, Toan stood up and toasted me with a glass of Chinese apple wine. He told me how much he and his friends loved me, and how much they were going to miss me, because we'd become family.

Another friend stood beside him, raised his glass, and said, quite sincerely, "I love you, Ben." One by one, others followed suit. One friend tapped his chest, made a heart shape with his hands, and pointed at me.

I'd been raised in a family that rarely expressed their emotions. I'd worked hard to become more expressive in my own relationships – but I had no response for such an intense, spontaneous outpouring of love. It was beyond anything I'd ever experienced. I was simply overwhelmed, and fumbled through the moment until it passed.

If I could change one thing from those months in Sapa, it would be to give my friends the response they deserved, to tell them that I loved them, too – because I did, and do. Sapa had become as much a home to me as anywhere in the world, and my friends there had indeed become like family.

Toan said he wanted me to become their elder brother. I was honoured and, naturally, said yes.

Only later did I realise he had a strange little ceremony in mind, which involved drinking shots of rice wine laced with each other's blood. I was somewhat less enthusiastic about that part.

RAMBLE ON

My final day in Vietnam was also Dominique's birthday.

Dominique had planned to come back to Sapa so we could celebrate her birthday together, but she'd had visa trouble. Instead we decided to meet across the border in China a few days later, on our way to Tibet.

May and her friends were disappointed that Dominique wouldn't be coming back to Sapa. May told me I should smuggle her into China with me, so that Dominique could see her "Hmong sister" again – then she realised that Dominique and I would probably prefer to have some time alone when we were finally reunited.

Dominique was having a quiet birthday in Bali with her girlfriend. I'd spent some time in Bali and had some local friends there. One was wonderful enough to surprise Dominique with a cake, card, and flowers for me, and she was delighted.

A few evenings earlier, a Parisian family had been dining at Charlie's, and I'd enlisted their help to write a romantic message in French for Dominique's birthday card. They didn't speak English well enough to understand the message I'd written, so they created their own – something sweet and sappy about fireworks inflaming our hearts, and enduring the solitude of long tropical nights with the memory of her smile.

I used an online translator to translate some other cute phrases into bad French, and wrote them out on large blue cards: "Happy birthday, Dominique!", "I miss you!", "Come back to Sapa!", and, "I love you more than 42 buffaloes and a chicken!"

May, Zao, Pang, and Chu came with me to the lake where Dominique and I had first met, and we took each other's photos posing with the signs I'd made. Zao picked some flowers, used them to make a love-heart on the grass, and lay beside it holding one of the signs.

A Kinh friend took a picture of May, Pang, and I standing together by the flower beds – the only picture the three of us have together. I took May's portrait as she sat by the lake, smiling in the last of the afternoon light.

For the second time, Toan closed the restaurant at the Yellow Dragon and organised a farewell banquet with the staff. He booked the largest karaoke room in town, and twenty Kinh and Hmong friends came together one last time. Somehow, Toan had even convinced Huong to come all the way back from her village for the party.

I was happy to see her again, and Toan was over the moon.

May, Zao, Chu, and the other Hmong girls couldn't sing karaoke because they couldn't read the lyrics on the screen, but they came anyway. I recorded a video of us all singing 'Happy Birthday' together for Dominique, which I later sent her with the photos we'd taken by the lake.

After a few drinks, Toan took me aside. He was distressed and embarrassed that he didn't have enough money to pay me for my work at the Yellow Dragon. It didn't matter, I said. He'd already given me more than I could have hoped for.

When the time came to say goodbye, several of my Kinh friends cried, and hugged me, and told me they loved me.

I drove May and two of her friends back to Sapa's main square on my motorbike. It was a very typically Vietnamese experience – four of us piled on one bike with no helmets, in the pouring rain. The girls got off at Cau May Street, and I watched them disappear into the rain.

Until that moment, my sense of loss at leaving Sapa had been balanced by my excitement to see Dominique again. Suddenly it hit me – all of the wonderful things that had happened that evening had happened for the last time. One of the most beautiful chapters in my life was closing, and the next day a new chapter would begin.

From that moment forward, all of those paths that had crossed so happily with my own – May's, Toan's, and all of our friends' – would diverge. I didn't know if or when those paths would ever cross again.

Toan was taking me to Lao Cai the next morning. I've never liked goodbyes, and wanted to leave as quickly as possible – but Toan had other ideas. I climbed onto the back of his motorbike, and he took me on a victory lap around the heart of Sapa.

Sapa was a small town and, by that time, it had become impossible for me to walk down the street without bumping into people I knew. We saw friends everywhere we went, and stopped to see a few in particular. Toan had arranged everything in advance. One friend, who worked in a restaurant on Cau May Street, had packed a lunch for me. Others gave me gifts and personal messages.

I was hoping to see May one last time, but she wasn't on the corner near the Yellow Dragon. Toan and I found her by the side of the road, walking down to Charlie's to look for me. She had three gifts for me, the kinds of things she normally sold to tourists – a bag, a purse, and a beautiful indigo shirt covered in elaborate embroidery and batik work. I have them here with me now, as I write.

It was a quiet, casual goodbye, with a hug and smiles, as if we'd be seeing each other again soon. There were no tears or grand sentimental gestures. I could never have imagined the circumstances under which I'd next hear

May's voice.

I climbed back onto the bike, Toan took me for a final spin around the lake, and then Sapa was behind us.

It was August – one of the most beautiful months in Sapa – and the weather was warm. The rice terraces which had been stark and muddy on my arrival were now lush and green before the harvest.

For the past week or so, Toan had been talking about getting tattoos together. Few Vietnamese people wore tattoos, and this would be his first. He'd asked me to design one especially for him: a snarling lion's head he wanted tattooed across his heart. For myself, I chose a simple, five-pointed Vietnamese star.

We'd set aside a few hours in Lao Cai to have the work done – but when the moment arrived, Toan began acting strangely. I knew he didn't want me to leave, but there was something else that I didn't understand. I had the same feeling I'd had on the evening we'd first met – that I didn't really know him at all.

We stopped at a tattoo parlour. Toan had a brief conversation with the artist before turning to me and telling me it was impossible, because there wasn't enough time. I didn't need to understand Vietnamese to see his heart wasn't in it.

One of my students had caught the bus down from Sapa to say goodbye. The three of us found a café with a view across the river to China. We sat and talked in the sun for a few hours – and then there was the station, plenty of hugs, a few tears, and I was gone.

Toan's strange behaviour continued after my departure. When I asked about Charlie's, he became evasive, and I later learned that Charlie's had closed. Toan was embarrassed, but offered no explanation.

The real reason, I soon discovered, was the same reason I'd been living in Sapa in the first place: Huong. Toan and Huong were getting married. I realised they must have come to some arrangement on my final evening in Sapa: no tattoos, and no Charlie's.

Instead of helping their relationship, as Toan had hoped, I'd become a major stumbling block to it. Was that part of the reason why Huong had left Sapa – because Toan and I had been spending every evening at Charlie's?

I don't know: I never asked.

In any case, there was no need for Toan's embarrassment – I was delighted for them both. Charlie's had marked a special moment in our lives, but it was over. Our paths were leading us in other directions now: Toan's with Huong, and mine with Dominique.

I didn't need a tattoo to remember him by – there was no way I could ever forget.

I remembered how I'd felt three months earlier, when Sapa was just a name, and I'd been looking forward to leaving Vietnam. Now I could hardly believe I was leaving at all. I had no way of knowing that my Sapa story was far from over – in fact, it was only just beginning.

A LONG WAY FROM HOME

Dominique and I had felt something special in Vietnam, and were both really looking forward to seeing each other again – but in reality, we didn't know each other very well. We'd spent ten days together in undemanding circumstances, and exchanged a long series of emails – that was all.

Now, suddenly, we were living together on the road. We were with one another twenty-four hours a day in an unfamiliar and constantly changing environment. There were endless decisions to be made – where to go, how to get there, what to do, how to arrange food and accommodation – in a country where even the simplest things could be incredibly difficult.

Every relationship is a gamble – but Dominique and I went all-in on the first hand.

It wasn't like dating someone at home, where we

might see each other once or twice a week in safe, comfortable situations, and would come to know each other gradually. We never had time to prepare our best selves in advance, and couldn't cancel a date when we didn't feel up to it. We leapt straight in at the deep end. It wasn't always fun, easy, or comfortable. We saw each other at our worst – when we were sick, exhausted, or simply overwhelmed.

What's more, Dominique's background as a French Canadian was very different to my own – we didn't share the same cultural points of reference, or even the same ways of thinking.

In China, Dominique and I came to know each other extremely well, extremely quickly – and we were amazing together. Our relationship was everything I'd hoped it would be, and more. What began as a journey to Tibet became the adventure of a lifetime, and we experienced things that most people could only dream of.

Dominique and I covered thousands of kilometres through some of the most incredible landscapes on Earth, travelling overland from coastal China all the way up to the north face of Everest, and down to the tropical beaches of the Arabian Sea. We explored temples, deserts, caves, glaciers, ruins, plunging gorges, and the immense silent valleys of Tibet. We came face-to-face with yaks, pandas, and hordes of monkeys, and stalked wild rhinos through the cool shade of the forests.

We hitchhiked across barren plateaus, and lost

ourselves in the labyrinthine slums of some of the world's most crowded cities. We ate moon cakes at the mid-autumn festival in rural China, shucked great mounds of corn in a remote Tibetan compound, watched elephants playing soccer in Nepal, and painted murals in India. We were televised, and mingled with Bollywood stars. We huddled together on the roof of a bus as it wound its way through the Himalayas.

We danced with locals in smoky mountain huts, played guitar in the sun, and sang songs around campfires. We saw strange gods and animal sacrifices, sat before the Dalai Lama, and stood in silence at some of the most sacred places on Earth. We witnessed human bodies being burned, or sliced apart and fed to the vultures. We hiked through forests of fluttering prayer flags, and traced koras around distant monasteries and wind-swept stupas. We watched the monolithic Potala Palace rise above the rooftops of Lhasa in the last light of day.

We were delayed, stranded, hospitalised, cheated, threatened, harassed, half-frozen, and starved of oxygen. We endured endless bus rides and each other's bad jokes. We ate all kinds of strange food, and made love at every opportunity. It was life, and young love, at its very best.

By the time Dominique and I reached the southern tip of India, eight intense months later, I'd begun to miss the deeper friendships and sense of home I'd felt in Sapa. Dominique and I turned north again, and spent the monsoon season living in an idyllic Nepali village we'd found nestled amongst the Himalayan foothills.

There were no cars or motorbikes in the village. Sometimes in the evening, the clouds parted to reveal a soul-stirring view across the valley to the Annapurna massif, a long line of colossal, craggy snow-covered monsters.

In the village, Dominique introduced herself as my wife, and wore the local tokens of marriage – a long necklace of red and gold, a red bindi on her forehead, and a smear of red tikka paste at the crest of her hair.

We rented a large but simple room cluttered with pictures of Hindu gods, where we practiced yoga together every morning. We became close to a local family, spent our evenings at their home, and soon learned to speak Nepali. Dominique taught French and English at the local schools, and I spent my days writing a novel I'd begun in Sapa.

Our lives fell into the rhythm of the sun, and we disconnected from the outside world. For months, we barely left the village. There was a tiny Internet café with a painfully slow connection, and we were rarely online. I'd given my phone away to a Nepali friend, and had no intention of buying another.

It was a magical time, but we knew it couldn't last forever. We'd already begun making plans for our future together. Dominique made no secret of the fact that she wanted to spend her life with me. She planned to return home to Quebec City the following year to resume her studies, and wanted me to come with her.

After the freedom we'd enjoyed, we knew it wouldn't be easy to return to the Western world, but Dominique and I were determined to do it our way. We'd transplant our Nepali life to French Canada, as best we could – a simple life, in a little place with a vegetable garden and space to practice yoga. Dominique would study, while I'd learn French, get a job, and publish my novel.

Dominique's parents both came to visit us. They were wonderful people, and were looking forward to having us there in Quebec.

Our Nepali visas were expiring and we had to leave the village we loved, but new adventures lay ahead.

Our last full day in the village was Dominique's birthday – exactly one year since my final day in Vietnam. This time, we were able to celebrate together. I'd organised a treasure hunt which led her through the lanes and pathways of the village for the last time. She followed a trail of clues between the homes of our friends and the places we loved. It was a bittersweet day, tinged with the sadness of departure.

The next day we took a bus to the Nepali capital, Kathmandu, to organise our Indian visas. The everyday reality of village life was suddenly reduced to a sweet and distant memory, just as Sapa had been.

For three months after leaving Sapa, I'd had little contact with my Hmong and Kinh friends there. Facebook – our main point of connection – had been blocked in China. We'd begun messaging each other again over the past nine months, while Dominique and I were in Nepal and India, but our conversations were limited. The Internet connections we found were rarely good enough to support video chat, and – despite my best efforts to teach them – most of my friends in Vietnam could still read and write very little English.

Toan and Huong had married, and were pregnant with their first child. Two other Kinh friends had moved to Hanoi, and named me godfather to their firstborn son. My friends in Sapa were constantly asking when Dominique and I were getting married, and when we were coming back to visit.

On arrival in Kathmandu, Dominique and I took a room in a cosy little guesthouse in a quieter part of the city, and I checked my messages. That's when I received the message that stopped my world, and changed my life forever.

It was a single line from Zao which read:

"hmong boy sell may in china
is very sad to know this"

COME PICK ME UP

Exactly one year earlier, after leaving Sapa and before my rendezvous with Dominique, I'd spent a few days alone in China, and had gone hiking through an area known as the Dragon's Backbone.

In many ways, the Dragon's Backbone was quite similar to Sapa – a series of simple minority villages scattered between spectacular rice terraces on the flanks of forested mountains. I carried very little, finding my food and accommodation in the villages.

The Dragon's Backbone was wonderful – except for one thing. Everywhere I went, I saw masses of garbage strewn along the trail. Other tourists, who had also come to enjoy the area's rugged beauty had been unthinkingly destroying it with their litter. At every turn, I was confronted by empty bottles, soft-drink cans, and plastic food packaging.

Often, the hardest thing about solving a problem is making up your mind to do so.

The Dragon's Backbone was a gated park with an entrance fee. They should have somebody to clean this up, I thought – but they didn't.

I didn't want to let it upset me, so I tried to ignore it. The best and worst thing about us, as human beings, is our adaptability. It's amazing how quickly we can accept even the most horrendous things as just another part of the landscape, and simply move on with our lives.

I was soon so accustomed to seeing rubbish around me that I became half-blind to it. Then an empty plastic bag fluttering by the side of the trail caught my eye, and I suddenly realised I had another option: I could do something about it.

I picked up the bag and began to fill it. By the time it was full, I'd found another bag – and another.

As soon as I began picking up the garbage, I saw that the area was even more of a mess than I'd realised. Instead of turning away, I took it as a challenge, and it was incredibly satisfying to see what a difference I could make.

Over the next two days, I must have cleared the garbage of hundreds, if not thousands, of people – and the trail was utterly transformed. The Dragon's Backbone was a remote corner of the world I'd never seen before and would likely never see again, but it was a wonderful feeling to leave the area looking even better than I'd found it.

From then on, every time I went hiking, I took a bag. Dominique soon took up the habit, too. Wherever we went, we'd collect garbage, and we always had a wonderful reaction from the locals. In areas of little or no environmental awareness, we were often met with bemused bewilderment, but it didn't take long for people to understand what we were doing, and to see what a difference we were making.

Locals often greeted us with great big grins and two thumbs up. In one village, we were received with applause. Some people wanted to photograph us with our bags, and those who could speak a little English couldn't praise us enough for what we were doing.

The best reaction of all, however, came from those who would simply take a bag and join in.

Some locals found it amusing that Dominique and I had apparently come halfway around the world just to pick up garbage off someone else's land. It didn't matter to me whose land it was – it was merely a problem that needed solving, which nobody else seemed to be doing anything about. I didn't want to argue about whose problem it was, nor did I want to shame or blame anyone. I was in a position to do something about it, so I did. It was that simple.

I soon realised that the biggest difference Dominique and I made came not from the garbage we collected, but from the people who saw us collect it. Our actions had a ripple effect. They made us a walking advertisement for a set of values which were important to me, but which

I'd rarely expressed so visibly.

Many other people had the same values, but weren't taking action. Some people had never thought about these things at all. By the simple act of picking up litter, Dominique and I brought all of these people together, and – in that particular time and place – set a new standard for behaviour.

A culture is merely the sum of our individual actions, and – in our own small way – we were helping to create a new culture.

There was a part of me that had always felt a vague sense of helplessness at the state of the world. It seemed there were so many problems, and so few people who genuinely cared to solve them. Now, however, my perspective changed dramatically. I saw that there were in fact many people who cared, but few who took action.

For too long, I'd been one of the people standing by, wishing and hoping for change without actually doing anything. Ultimately, I realised, action was the only thing that mattered.

The moment I began to take action, however insignificant, my lingering sense of helplessness vanished, and I became another person.

There was a cave outside our Nepali village, which was accessible only with a local guide. Our guide was a young Nepali man named Bimal. When Dominique and I saw the cave was full of garbage, we began picking it up, as was our habit. I was deeply impressed when, without a word, Bimal began to help. I was far more impressed, however, when I learned Bimal had taken up the habit and, months later, was still collecting any garbage he found in the cave.

It was a matter of pride, I realised. Bimal saw the cave every day, and he knew it was filthy – but he was a guide, not a garbage collector, and it would have been an insult to his pride to pick up after others. However, once Dominique and I had normalised the act of picking up garbage and had cleaned parts of the cave, Bimal's pride shifted – and grew. He was no longer guiding people through a cave full of garbage, but a cave he'd helped clean with his own hands. The cleanliness of that cave became part of his identity. The pride which had once worked against him, was now working for him – to everyone's benefit.

I could feel the same change within myself. I became more aware of the effects we all have, for better or for worse, upon the world. I saw what a difference an individual could truly make.

I was no longer someone who travelled the world, leaving only footprints. Even as the act of picking up other people's garbage humbled me, I felt a stronger sense of connection to – and responsibility for – the world I lived in. I felt a healthy sense of growing pride in myself, in my immediate environment, and in the difference I was making, however small.

I'd seen the world's problems as huge and overwhelming, and couldn't imagine how I could possibly make a difference against them. Now I realised that so many of those problems were created by individuals, in individual measures, and they could be solved the same way.

I'd been searching for some sense of purpose to my travels. I'd imagined it would be some large and complex endeavour, but now it all seemed so simple. All I had to do was to stop searching, and start acting.

From that one simple act of picking up garbage, a positive change flowed through every aspect of my life – how I thought, what I bought, how I ate, who I met, and what we spoke about.

Although it might sound comical, I knew that picking up garbage was just a beginning. It signalled a change within me, giving me a new approach to life, and setting me on a new path. I felt more aware, more responsible, and more confident to deal with whatever life might throw at me.

Life was wonderful. I felt a sense of purpose and connectedness, and shared my days with an amazing woman who loved and supported me. I had some money in the bank, and had almost finished my first novel.

Then I received Zao's message, and my world stopped.

EASY WAY OUT

I'm sure you can remember where you were when the Twin Towers collapsed in New York. When the unimaginable and seemingly impossible suddenly becomes cold hard reality, when you're suddenly thrown from one path onto another, the sense of shock and dislocation etches itself clearly in the mind.

When I received Zao's message, I was sitting on the bed in our room at the guesthouse in Kathmandu, and Dominique was in a chair by the window. I read her the message, and we both sat stunned. May – my friend, and Dominique's "Hmong sister" – had been sold in China.

Who was the "Hmong boy" that Zao referred to? How could he have taken May from Sapa, and across an international border? Who had bought her, and what did they intend to do with her? How did Zao know, and where was May now?

None of it made any sense to me. To have witnessed a stranger being trafficked in northern Thailand was one thing; to know that a personal friend was, at that very moment, being carried to some unknown fate – that was something else entirely. My world had suddenly lurched in a direction I'd never imagined possible.

May had countless friends. She was well-known to many of the locals in Sapa and the surrounding villages. She already had over three hundred international friends on the Facebook profile I'd helped her set up barely a year earlier – most of them, I assumed, were tourists she'd taken trekking.

I was in an unusual position, at the intersection of two worlds. Having lived in Sapa, I had local contacts and knowledge that few other foreigners had. As a Westerner, I also had access to resources and contacts beyond Sapa, which the locals didn't have.

Only a handful of other people – half a dozen, perhaps – were in the same position. If anyone could help May now, surely it was one of us.

Of that handful of people, I imagined that most had jobs, families, or other commitments. I was very likely the only one who was completely free – and, if the past year had taught me anything at all, it was the true importance of action. I had to do something.

I had the time and money to go back to Sapa, to get a better understanding of the situation. I could find out if there was any chance to help May, however small.

If nothing else, Dominique and I could spend time with May's friends, who must have been crushed by May's disappearance. We could visit Toan and our Kinh friends, too, and meet my Vietnamese godson for the first time.

It was only a short hop from Kathmandu to Hanoi. Nothing could have been simpler – but we didn't do it. We never even considered it as a serious possibility. I thought I'd been ready for anything, but this was just too much.

Gradually, Dominique and I began to convince each other that it wasn't our problem, and there was nothing we could do. Slowly, the world began to move again, even if it was now spinning slightly off-centre.

Sapa had been such a special place for both of us. Without Sapa, Dominique and I would never have met. All of the wonderful things that had happened over the past year were a direct result of that meeting – but now everything had changed.

With May's disappearance, the memories we'd cherished suddenly darkened. With my own inaction, I lost the sense of self-respect and empowerment I'd gained over the past year. A shadow fell through our lives.

Again, I'd been tested, just as I'd been tested that afternoon in northern Thailand. Again, I'd failed, and left a young woman in the clutches of her captors. Again, I'd taken the wrong path – I'd taken the easy way out, turning a blind eye to a friend in her moment of greatest need.

Dominique and I pretended that the news of May's abduction didn't really affect us. Zao's message had left a tiny pinhole in our lives, that was all. We convinced ourselves that we could continue living our lives just as we had before – and so we did. We spent the afternoon at our favourite Nepali café, eating chocolate cake.

It was a long time before I realised how much of our love and happiness, and how much of my own sense of self-worth, were leaking out through that tiny hole. It was months before I realised how empty and misshapen my life had become as a result of that inaction.

FROM A BALANCE BEAM

In 1978, before my parents were married, they'd travelled overland from Kathmandu to London. They'd been in Afghanistan when war erupted, and Iran during the prelude to the revolution. They'd passed through Moscow in the depths of the Cold War, and crossed the wall in Berlin.

The long journey from East to West appealed to my sense of adventure. Dominique and I had already travelled thousands of kilometres overland together, and now decided to continue all the way to her home in French Canada.

It was a journey that would dwarf the one we'd made already, reaching beyond even the journey my parents had made. After crossing half of Asia and the entire length of Europe, we'd still have to find our way across the Atlantic Ocean. We didn't know how it could be done, but we were determined to give it our best shot. Dominique was to resume her studies in Quebec the following September, which gave us twelve months.

In Delhi, Dominique and I had an unexpected opportunity to buy a van from a fellow traveller, and we jumped at the chance. I'd previously owned two campervans – in Australia, and in New Zealand – and they had both been wonderful. It was an amazing way to travel, and an experience I wanted to share with Dominique.

On the very first day, Dominique and I began to regret our decision. Driving in India was a harrowing experience. Within the first hour we found ourselves gridlocked in a narrow Delhi alleyway, with a festival on one side and an approaching demonstration on the other.

The streets were a seething sea of motorbikes, trucks, taxis, cycle rickshaws, pedestrians, men carrying heavy loads on their heads, and absurdly overloaded carts drawn by hand, bicycle, and bullock. The roads were cracked and broken, the traffic was relentless, and the rules seemed non-existent. Vehicles came gushing in from every direction, surging in waves through any gap. Dominique had her first panic attack in the passenger seat, and I didn't know how to help her.

We soon realised that crossing borders with the van would be far more complicated and expensive than we'd imagined, and the van itself turned out to be a lemon. The grand cross-continental journey we'd envisaged became an excruciating hobble between the mechanics' workshops of northern India, where we were cheated mercilessly. One mechanic, we later realised, had not only stolen parts from the van, but had charged us for the privilege. We found ourselves lost amongst a tangle of narrow, hair-raising roads in the Himalayan foothills, where one wrong turn could mean a long, violent tumble to our deaths.

By the time we reached Dharamshala, I was ill with fever, and we were both exhausted. Dominique and I decided enough was enough, and agreed to sell the van – only to discover we didn't legally own it. A crucial document had been withheld by its former owner, an unscrupulous second-hand car dealer in Delhi. We had little alternative but to limp all the way back to Delhi and sell him the keys for an enormous loss.

Under other circumstances, our Indian van experience wouldn't have been such a disaster. Dominique and I had wasted a little time and lost some money, that was all. We could have laughed it off, and marked it down as yet another wild chapter in the story of our lives.

But something had changed. I'd lost my balance, and was feeling deeply unsettled. I didn't know what the problem was, and I didn't know how to talk about it. My life had been going so well, but now I felt as though everything was coming apart somehow. For the first time, I found myself arguing with Dominique – which only left me angry at myself, and made the situation worse.

Most of the time, things were still wonderful between us – but a strange new note had entered our relationship, and I didn't understand where it had come from.

Dominique's family were having a special gathering in Canada in March, and asked her to join them. Instead of the year we'd planned to spend travelling to Quebec, that left her only a few months, and so we changed our plans.

I decided not to go to Canada with Dominique in March.

Moving to another country to be with someone you love is a huge step, especially when the language and culture are different to your own. I'd never been to Quebec, and knew only two things about it – that the winter there was long and bitterly cold, and that the people spoke French. I'd never enjoyed the cold, and couldn't speak French.

I knew our lives would be very different there – Dominique and I spoke about it often. She'd be studying, and I'd have to find work. There were plenty of unknowns. It would be a leap of faith, which I was more than willing to make for Dominique – but I wasn't quite ready yet.

It had been over three years since I'd left a steady job in Australia and begun travelling through Asia. They'd been three intense years of love, friendship, and adventure, and my experiences had affected me in deep and lasting ways. They'd led me to the woman that I loved and, one day, intended to marry. Soon they would lead me to a new life on a continent I'd never even seen.

I should have been happy – but somewhere, amongst that wealth of experience, something was wrong. I needed a little time to sift through my experiences, to make sense of them, and understand how they'd shaped me. I needed time to regain my balance and prepare for our life together in Quebec.

Dominique knew me better than anyone, and seemed to understand. She agreed it would be a good idea if she spent some time at home with her family first, and I went to join her there later.

It wasn't the first time we'd spent time apart, and we were quite comfortable doing so. On three occasions in Nepal and India, Dominique had entered yoga or meditation retreats, and I'd spent weeks alone on the beach, or in the mountains. I enjoyed having a little time to myself, and felt it was healthy to have breathing space within the relationship.

Dominque and I flew together as far as Europe, spent two weeks with friends in France and Spain, and then she went home to Quebec.

TIME TO THINK

Before her departure, Dominique and I had spent several days with Dai, a Catalan paraglider we'd met in Nepal.

Dai was a slim man, with warm, friendly eyes. He'd built a lovely home and garden in the hills north of Barcelona, where he grew much of his own food. Dai lived a simple life in tune with nature – just the kind of life Dominique and I hoped to create for ourselves in Quebec.

After Dominique left for Canada, Dai asked me what my plans were.

I didn't have much money left. I was thinking about buying a bicycle and spending a few weeks riding around southern Spain. It would be a cheap and healthy way to spend a little time, and would give me the space I needed to think. I imagined myself deep in reflection as the kilometres wheeled past.

"Come with me," Dai said. "I have something that might help you."

He led me downstairs to the garage. In a dark corner I saw a silver bicycle, its frame covered in colourful stickers – the flags of many different countries. Though he'd never before mentioned it, I learned that Dai had spent three years as a touring cyclist. He'd covered 35,490km around the Americas, from Tierra del Fuego in the south to Quebec City in the north. It seemed fitting that Quebec had been the end of his journey, as it would be mine.

Dai lifted the frame and handed it to me.

"For three years, this was my wife," he said. "Now, she is yours."

Dai's cycling days were behind him. He gave me everything – the bicycle, clip shoes (which were a perfect fit), saddlebags, locks, and a small tent. I was overwhelmed by his generosity.

I started riding two days later, with zero training and minimal preparation. The locals who saw the bicycle's myriad flags must have thought it strange that someone who had apparently cycled halfway around the world should now be struggling with their relatively low hills.

I soon built up my strength, ultimately pedalling all the way across Spain to the Algarve, in southern Portugal.

The days passed quickly, and the kilometres flew by. I slowly became aware of how deeply May's disappearance had disturbed me, and how profoundly my sense of self-worth had been shaken by my failure to act in Kathmandu.

The original problem had now become compounded by my own guilt and shame. It seemed somehow easier to accept my own weakness and to write the episode off as a failure than to actually do something about it. I rationalised, and told myself what I needed to hear.

I told myself it was too late to do anything to help May – any trail left by her kidnapper would have long since gone cold. In any case, I was walking a different path now, which was leading me in the opposite direction around the globe.

I compromised with my conscience, and settled for a lesser version of myself.

Returning the bicycle to Dai, I went to visit Marta and Fausto, two wonderful human beings who lived amongst the mountains of northern Italy. Marta and Fausto were both painters – she painted murals, and he painted houses.

I'd met the couple two years earlier, when I'd first arrived in Vietnam. They'd also been travelling northwards along the coast and, although we'd never exchanged contact details, we'd bumped into each other constantly – in Hoi An, Ninh Binh, Hanoi, and finally Sapa. Marta joked about having microchipped me, to make me easier to follow.

Marta and Fausto were lovely people who radiated health and a joy for life. They'd shared my love for Sapa, and had also extended their Vietnamese visas to stay there for an extra fortnight. When I wasn't teaching, the three of us had explored Sapa and its surrounding villages together.

Fausto was a wonderful storyteller. As we explored Sapa, he'd told me stories from his life with Marta. My favourite story was about an old hospital outside their hometown – a large, rambling structure, half-hidden amongst the forested mountains.

Several years earlier, Marta and Fausto had seen the hospital from a distance while out hiking. Marta had been enchanted with the grand old building, and said she wished it was her home.

It was just an offhand remark, and an impossible fantasy. The hospital had long since been condemned, and was falling apart. Local youths would go there to drink, smashing bottles in its desolate rooms.

Marta forgot her comment almost immediately – but Fausto didn't. Every day for weeks, he went to the old hospital after work. After selecting a large downstairs room with a fireplace, he cleaned out the masses of accumulated debris, swept the floors, and painted the walls. Finally, he brought in rugs, furniture, and utensils from his own house, and prepared a lavish meal for two.

Fausto had a date with Marta that evening. Instead of picking her up from her home, he arranged for a mutual friend to collect Marta and deliver her, blindfolded – along mountain roads, and through the woods – to the old hospital, where he was putting the finishing touches on his creation.

The friend left, and Marta removed the blindfold to find Fausto there with a homecooked, candlelit dinner in the freshly decorated house of her dreams.

Needless to say, the date went well.

The following evening, when Fausto returned after work to collect his furniture, he discovered that Marta had also made a clandestine visit to the old hospital. She'd painted a large pink-and-gold flower on the wall to thank him for their evening together.

On my first day in Marta and Fausto's hometown, they took me to see the old hospital. It was a beautiful place, and the mountain air reminded me of our time together in Sapa.

Marta and Fausto had known May, and I'd told them of her disappearance. We decided to paint a mural there together in the old hospital – a mural in remembrance of May and Sapa. We returned the next day with paints, brushes, and a picnic lunch, and set to work.

We painted mountains covered in endless rice terraces, with a deep, misty valley between. At the centre of the image was a large golden sun, bursting through the clouds that wreathed the sky above.

It was amazing to see Marta at work, and how quickly and effortlessly she could create something so beautiful. I'd always loved painting, though my own work was crude and clumsy beside hers.

In the foreground, I painted a picture of May in her traditional Black Hmong costume. She was turned away, as if preparing to descend into the valley, and smiling back over her shoulder. I drew her face from the portrait I'd taken by the lake during my last days in Sapa.

The mural was my way of saying goodbye to May – of putting the past behind me, so I could move forward with my own life.

Six days later, I crossed the Atlantic for the first time, to begin a new life with Dominique in Quebec. We had so much to catch up on.

G*PSY FADED

It was almost two years since Dominique and I had first met in Sapa. We'd shared so much in those two years, and I felt as though we could talk about anything.

As soon as I arrived in Quebec, I realised that something was terribly wrong. The Dominique I found there was not the one I had known. She was cool and distant, and introduced me half-heartedly to her friends. Just a few days earlier, she'd been speaking about marriage and children; now she barely spoke to me at all. I struggled desperately to understand what was happening.

It took Dominique two torturous weeks to muster up her courage, and then she threw me out of the house.

To clarify, this story isn't about Dominique, or our relationship. It would be both unfair and unnecessary to sift through the ashes here. Dominique is a wonderful person, and I feel privileged and grateful to have shared such a special time in my life with her. The only reason I've included her in this story at all is to explain the effect that the end of our relationship had on my life.

It's a time I've rarely spoken about, even to my closest friends. While I have very mixed feelings about sharing it here, it's a crucial part of the story, and it would be dishonest to tell this story any other way.

As it stands, the only thing I've changed is Dominique's name. Hers is one of several names in this story that have been changed for various reasons.

Neither of us were perfect. With the benefit of hindsight, there were clear warning signs, and there were certainly things I could have done better. At the time, though, the end of our relationship came as a bolt from the blue, and I was utterly unprepared for it.

I found myself, literally overnight, in a situation I would never have imagined possible: with no home, no money, and no job, in a city where I couldn't even speak the language.

How did it feel?

Imagine the sudden shock of a heavy door slamming in your face, and the pain of having all ten fingers caught in that door. Now imagine the confusion you'd feel when you realised that door had been slammed shut intentionally, by someone you loved and trusted deeply. Then imagine the sense of loss you'd feel in knowing your hopes and dreams for the future all lay on the other side of that door, in a place you'd never see or set foot again.

Suffice to say, it didn't feel good. If I'd been feeling unbalanced before, I was now hurtling over the edge. If the news of May's abduction had stopped my world, this smashed it to pieces.

NO FUTURE

When I was twenty-one, I'd fallen for a woman ten years my senior. She was a single mother who lived in a little house on the hill above my hometown.

She and I spent long evenings together. Sometimes she'd recite poetry, or sing and play softly for me on her guitar, while her child slept in the next room. We'd sit and speak for hours, as the pale light of dawn came trickling into the house.

Ultimately, that woman chose not to pursue a relationship with me, because I was just too young. I hadn't been particularly upset with her decision, because I knew that she was right. She needed a man to be a father to her child, and I was still half a child myself.

A short time later, that woman left to live in another city, and we never saw or spoke to each other again. I've never forgotten what she told me when we met for the last time.

She believed there was something unusual about me – a fiery passion for life which very few people had. At the age of twenty-one, she said, that passion was already a rare thing. If I could keep that flame alive for another decade, that would really be something amazing. She didn't know anyone her own age who still had that burning passion for life.

She spoke sincerely, and I was flattered. Afterwards, when I thought back on her comments, they made me smile. What could possibly change me? I thought.

Since then, I'd travelled through dozens of countries, and seen and done incredible things. I'd known love and heartbreak. I'd met countless wonderful people, many of whom had also commented on my passion and enthusiasm for life. For nine long years, I'd learned and grown. I'd changed in many ways – but I'd never let go of that flame.

Now, for the first time, I felt something fundamental shift in the very depths of my being.

My life had been more adventuresome than most, and I'd taken my share of risks. Those risks were based on a faith in other people, and a faith in my own judgement. Both of those things had now failed me in the most devastatingly painful way.

In a heartbeat, my passion and relentless optimism had vanished. The map of the world, where every point had whispered to me of endless adventures and friends still unknown, had fallen silent. I didn't want to go home, I had no interest in remaining where I was, and there was nowhere else I wanted to be. I didn't want to meet new people, and I didn't want to see the people I already knew.

The flame within me had been extinguished, and I no longer recognised myself at all. Unless I could find a way to relight that flame, I was just an empty shell, a deadweight on the world.

IN MY TIME OF NEED

The months that followed were the most difficult of my life.

I was adrift, cut loose from everything I'd known, and had no idea what would happen to me. There were times I thought I'd find myself living on the street, and I didn't really care.

There were few people around me – after all, I'd barely arrived in the country. Dominique had introduced me to almost everyone I knew in Quebec, and most of them vanished from my life the moment she did.

Others didn't know how to respond to my sudden reversal in fortune, and quietly stepped away. I didn't blame them – I wouldn't have known how to react, either.

I felt like a piece of garbage that had been casually dropped by the side of the trail. People who, under other circumstances, might have called themselves my friends no longer seemed to see me at all.

What would I have done, in their shoes? Would I have offered a helping hand to someone else in a similar situation? I didn't know if I would – I knew only that I never had. Intention meant little: action was the only true measure.

Sadly, I realised I'd never set my own needs aside to help someone more deserving, not in any meaningful way. How could I expect anyone else to do the same for me?

Yet some people did.

My family offered to buy me a flight home, but I chose not to take it. I didn't want them to see me in the state that I was in.

A friend decided I needed to get out of the city and clear my head. We drove along the coast for three days, camping wild by the Gulf of St Lawrence. I wasn't great company, but it meant a lot to me just knowing that someone cared.

The same friend helped me find a job that didn't require any French. It was nothing special – a minimum-wage job in a kitchen across the city – but it was something.

There was a clerical error at my job, and my first paycheck arrived a week late. As a backpacker, I was used to living cheaply, and now I'd really tightened my belt. Even so, I ran out of money completely. I didn't tell anyone, but it wasn't an easy thing to hide.

A friend insisted I take a cash prize of five hundred Canadian dollars she'd won in a competition at her office, and I don't know what I would have done without it. The same friend let me stay at her house for a short time, and helped arrange another place for me to live.

A friend of hers, whom I'd met only once, heard my story and offered me a place at her home. I found myself living on a folding couch in a small nook in the corner of her basement, with a bedsheet for a door and a bath towel for a curtain. I felt fortunate to have that much.

These people saved me – and not just in a material sense. It was a deeply humbling experience, and it made a world of difference to me just knowing I wasn't alone.

I lived in the basement for two months while I scraped a few dollars together and tried to work out my next step. I had to rebuild my life, but didn't know where to start.

Inspiration came from the most unlikely of places. One afternoon I found a copy of Kimya Dawson's latest album, 'Thunder Thighs', and put it on.

Kimya is an "anti-folk" singer whose lo-fi, lyrically-driven work often combines the political with the intensely personal. I loved her music and had been listening to it for many years, but this was the first time I'd heard her newest album.

Somewhere towards the end of a six-minute song about the 2010 oil spill in the Gulf of Mexico, Kimya let slip an innocuous little line that hit me like a bullet:

"It's time to define what success means to you."

That line knocked me flat. Kimya was right: it was time.

My experiences in Quebec had cut me deeply. I knew those experiences would change me in some profound and lasting way, and I was determined to change for the better. I refused to let my pain define me, or destroy my love and trust in other human beings.

For years, I'd been acutely aware of the effect that each of us has on this planet just by being here, and I'd been very conscious of minimising my negative impact. That attitude was no longer enough for me. Was that all I was capable of – of *not doing* something bad?

What if I did something *good?*

That was what success would mean to me – taking control of my life again, and shaping it in a way that made a positive difference in the lives of others. Though I didn't yet know what it might involve, I was determined to pay forward the generosity I'd received from my friends in Quebec.

I'd heard it said that the most generous people were often those who had the least to give. For the first time, I began to understand why that might be. I understood now what a huge difference a helping hand could make when you were in a difficult place. Though I had so little left to give, I would give it willingly in gratitude for the assistance I myself had received.

It was a resolution that was born in a dark place and it was to lead me somewhere darker still, to the darkest place I'd ever known – the world of human trafficking.

GOING TO CALIFORNIA

Eight years earlier, outside a hostel in Verona, I'd met an American woman named Jen. We'd grabbed a bite together and wandered the city for an hour or two, while Jen told me about a festival like no other.

Once a year, a strange and ephemeral city – Black Rock City – appeared like a mirage in the Nevada desert. People came from all over America and the world to be there. It wasn't a music festival – in fact, it was difficult to say exactly what it was.

They called it Burning Man.

At the centre of Black Rock City stood a towering human figure made of wood – the "Man". At the climax of the week-long festival, the Man was burned to the ground, and the entire city vanished soon after.

Jen had never been to the festival but she was excited to go, and I was fascinated by the way she described it. I told myself that if I ever spent a summer in North America, I'd go and see Burning Man for myself.

Jen and I parted ways at the end of the evening. We stayed in loose contact, exchanging occasional messages over the years – but we never saw each other again, and never spoke again about the festival.

From time to time, as I travelled the world, I met people who had been to Burning Man and tried to describe it to me. Dominique and I had spoken about it and, with only the vaguest idea of what we might expect there, this mysterious festival had become a distant dream of ours.

Now here I was in North America, for the first time. Burning Man was taking place at the end of the summer – but my life was different now, and I simply couldn't afford to go.

The entrance ticket alone was hundreds of dollars, and the entire journey from Quebec into the Nevada desert would cost far more than that. The idea was laughable – it was just another dream that had been sealed off by that slamming door.

Then something truly incredible happened.

Somewhere out there, scattered across the globe, was a small group of people I'd never met. They'd been to Burning Man several times, and planned to return that summer.

In addition to their festival tickets, they'd all chipped in to pay for a hotel room and rental car for two days in San Francisco, and ten days' rental on a large RV, which would be their transport and accommodation for the festival. The whole package would easily have cost them a thousand dollars each – a huge sum of money to me at that time.

At the last moment, one of those people was offered a job in Melbourne, and cancelled his trip to Burning Man.

Every year, in the weeks and months leading up to the festival, there's high demand for Burning Man tickets. No doubt there were hundreds, if not thousands, of people who would have happily paid good money for that package. Instead of selling it, however, he chose to give it away.

He could have given it to anyone. He offered it first to one of his friends, a woman named Jen – the same Jen I'd met all those years ago in Verona, and hadn't seen since.

Jen had been to Burning Man several times since I'd met her, but she couldn't go that year. She knew I'd been dreaming of Burning Man, and was aware of my situation in Quebec. She suggested that her friend offer the package to me – a complete stranger – and that's exactly what he did.

My new friends in Quebec were sceptical. It was a strange story, and seemed too good to be true. I barely knew Jen, and didn't know her friend at all. I had a safe place to live in Quebec, had begun meeting people there, and had even started scraping a little money together. If I was going to accept the offer, I'd have to leave my sanctuary and my new friends behind, and would have to gamble a large slice of my meagre savings on a flight to California.

The festival was an indulgence, a party for the privileged, and it would only last a week – what would I do when it was finished? I'd be almost broke again, this time in San Francisco – one of the most expensive cities in the United States, where I couldn't legally work. I was no longer in a position to be so reckless with money.

I'd taken a risk in coming to Quebec, and had been burned badly. In a practical sense, I couldn't afford to risk another flight to another unfamiliar corner of the world. In another, more meaningful sense, however, I couldn't afford not to. Until I could begin to trust my own judgement and start taking risks once more, I would never truly live again – and that was worse than anything that might happen to me in California.

If I'd given in to my fears and walked away from Toan on the night we'd first met in Sapa, I would have missed out on one of the most wonderful experiences of my life. Who knew what other adventures lay ahead, if only I had the courage to embrace them?

I bought my flight to San Francisco the same day.

Jen arranged everything for me. I never met her friend, and don't even know his name, but he gave me a much greater gift than he realised.

It was August when I left Quebec City – two years since I'd left Sapa, and a year since I'd received Zao's message.

I didn't know what Dominique was doing for her birthday that year, and I didn't want to think about it.

BLINKING LIGHTS (FOR ME)

Burning Man is a phenomenal explosion of colour and creativity across the vast, flat, white canvas of the Nevada desert. The festival is many different things to many different people – and for me, it was exactly what I needed. For the first time in months, I felt a spark of true excitement within me.

Black Rock City is hot by day, cold by night, and dusty all the time. All kinds of strange and fantastic things happen within it, and I can't possibly begin to describe them here.

The city's inhabitants include a broad cross-section of society, from straight-laced Silicon Valley tech workers wanting to let off a little steam, to those who find themselves on the fringes of society, who otherwise might not have a safe space to come together and express themselves.

The most important element of the festival, which makes everything else possible, is the creation of a non-judgemental culture. Under the banner of "radical inclusion", Burning Man lifted barriers I'd never even realised existed, because I'd never known a world without them. For the first time, I glimpsed the full spectrum of human creativity.

It was the perfect place to find inspiration, and I couldn't have asked for a better arrangement.

Jen's friends knew how to prepare for the extreme conditions of both the desert and the festival. Having been to Burning Man several times already, they were full of invaluable suggestions – but they were also a little jaded.

Only one other member of the group was, like me, a Burning Man "virgin", and shared the same level of energy and enthusiasm. The two of us leapt into the experience headfirst, and it was magical.

Every day, and every night, became an odyssey through an exotic land of surreal delights – a journey down the rabbithole and through the looking-glass, where nothing was quite as it seemed.

When we'd first passed through the gates of Black Rock City, we'd each been given a pocket-sized book which held the names and descriptions of the more structured experiences on offer at Burning Man. It was like a fantastic menu containing everything you could possibly imagine, and many things you couldn't.

Every morning, dazed and bleary, my friend and

I would flip through the book, fascinated by the possibilities on offer. We'd pick something and start cycling towards it – but we very rarely reached our chosen destination. There were simply too many things to see and do, and too many people to meet.

Each adventure led us in new and unexpected directions. Every time my friend and I became sidetracked, we faced a choice: we could struggle on towards our chosen destination, or we could make the most of whatever life threw at us.

We opened ourselves to the world, and embraced serendipity. It was good to have a plan – but it was also good to throw that plan away when circumstances changed. Invariably, what we discovered was worlds away from whatever we'd set out to find – but it was always something incredible. The experiences we found weren't listed in any books.

I faced the same dilemma in my own life. I'd been thrown off course, and realised it was senseless to struggle on with the same old fantasies. I could never go back to Dominique, and I could never replace her. The dreams we'd shared made no sense without her.

I was walking a new path now: it was time to accept that fact. It was time to stop and survey the landscape of my life from this new and unexpected position I found myself in, to see what opportunities it held for me, and to decide where I wanted to go from here.

My separation from Dominique, and the months that had followed, had been a soul-shattering experience

I wouldn't have wished on anyone. It was a black cloud that filled my world from one horizon to the other.

For the first time, I began to see a silver lining to my situation, however slight. The seed of inspiration that Kimya Dawson had planted now began to blossom.

I looked at the world with new eyes, questioned things I'd always taken for granted, and found countless new paths branching out on all sides. I began to see myself not as an isolated individual, but as a member of the global community.

Because my experience with Dominique had torn me apart so completely, I realised I had an opportunity to put myself back together in any way I chose – and there at Burning Man, I saw there were far more possibilities than I'd ever imagined.

I asked myself three questions:

Who did I want to be?

Where did I want to go? and,

What did I want to do?

WHERE DO I BEGIN

A year earlier, while Dominique and I had been living in Nepal, another backpacker had wandered into our little village, and into our lives.

Vanessa was – and is – a beautiful, generous, eternally positive human being. A decade my senior, Vanessa had also been born and raised in Australia. She'd left home in her late teens, and spent her adult life living and travelling around the world.

By the time we met, I'd spent five years abroad, which was more than most people I'd known. Vanessa had left Australia two decades earlier, and had barely been back since. As we came to know each other, I came to think of Vanessa as an older sister.

Vanessa carried her own energy with her, and could make herself at home anywhere. She'd recently bought a cosy little house in the mountains of southern California.

It was a peaceful place, with bobcats, coyotes, black bears, and even the occasional mountain lion prowling through the woods outside.

I felt lucky to have survived Quebec, and had no plans to return there. In fact, I didn't have any plans at all.

Vanessa and I found each other again at Burning Man. She invited me to come and stay with her in California for as long as I needed to get back on my feet, and I gratefully accepted.

I stayed with Vanessa for three weeks. There, at her little house in the forest, I took stock of my situation, and began to reevaluate my options.

The festivities I'd enjoyed at Burning Man were well and truly over. As if that hadn't been made clear enough by my rapidly dwindling savings, I'd broken a bone in my right foot whilst dancing, and could barely walk.

While Vanessa was at work, I spent long days by myself at her house in the woods. With little else to do, I began browsing through the files I had on my laptop.

I found the novel I'd poured so much of myself into, and had almost completed. It was something I'd been proud of, and I remembered how vitally important it had once seemed to me. Now, it was just a relic from my dead past – I set it aside, and never touched it again.

Instead, I found myself drawn back to the photos I'd taken in Asia. I found the pictures from my very first morning in Sapa, when it was still a new world to me, before it became my home. I flicked through the portraits of the grubby-faced children I'd met beside the trail.

I had no right to feel sorry for myself – my "rock bottom" was something those children could only dream of. Here I was, in a comfortable house with food on the table, the time to relax and reflect on my life, and a good friend who cared about me.

My suffering was a temporary thing, and comparatively mild. After three months, I was past the worst of it already, and knew I'd find my way back to a better place.

The children in my photographs had experienced deprivations I could scarcely imagine, and their futures held little hope for them. They'd never had the opportunities I had.

In the developed world, we had an abundance of wealth and material comfort. Even in my darkest moments, I'd always had electricity, running water, and a roof over my head. Yet I now lacked something more fundamental: a sense of meaning in my life. Without that, the rest held no value for me.

When I'd turned away from May in her moment of greatest need, I'd lost my self-respect, and it had cost me far more than I could have imagined. I understood now that if I wasn't living in accordance with my beliefs, then I wasn't really living at all.

When I looked back at my life, what would I most regret not having done?

I saw the photographs of May and her friends, and

thought of how May's future had been so brutally snatched away. I thought of the young girl lying helpless in the middle of the road in northern Thailand, and the two furious men I'd backed away from.

I was determined to do something good for other people, and it had to be something big enough to fill the strange new emptiness of my life. In a world of chaos and confusion, I wanted to do something pure and simple, something born from hope and love.

The best way to test a light is in darkness, and the best way to measure goodness is against something terrible. I knew of nothing darker than human trafficking – of people buying and selling each other like objects, abusing their power over other human beings for the sake of their own greed and lust.

I thought of all the friends who had helped me over the past months, and what a difference it had made just knowing that they cared. I wanted to pay their generosity forward, to be a true friend to the friend who needed it most.

I realised I already had the answers to my three questions: I wanted to be a good person, I wanted to go back to Asia, and I wanted to do everything I possibly could to help May. If I could, I would bring a little light into the darkest place I knew.

In Asia, I'd wasted my time waiting for a sense of greater purpose to guide my actions. Ultimately, I'd only discovered that sense of purpose after I began taking action – in that case, the simple act of picking up litter.

I saw now that I'd made the same mistake again: I'd hesitated to help May because it wasn't clear to me exactly how I could help her. I suddenly realised how little that mattered. That attitude had only held me back, giving me a convenient excuse for my inaction.

It was idiotic to tell myself there was nothing I could do to help May, if I'd never even tried. I was now determined to do something – all I'd have to do was to work out what that something was going to be.

It didn't matter what the best way forward might be: all I had to do was start moving. I didn't need to know where the path might lead me – I needed only to walk it, one step at a time. It didn't matter how senseless it might seem, what an utter waste of time and money it might be: if there was anything I could do to help May, I was going to do it.

I would certainly make mistakes. I would stumble, and I would fall – and I would get back up, and push forward. I didn't have to be perfect, and I didn't need anyone else's approval. All I had to do was to put one foot in front of the other.

How far was I willing to go?

I wasn't going to back away this time, not for anything. I was determined to follow this path to the end, wherever it might lead me. If that meant gambling my life for a chance to win May's freedom, then that's what I'd do.

There was nothing noble or selfless in my decision, and certainly nothing macho about it. It was a simple transaction, a chance to restore balance to May's life and my own.

The task that faced me would be like a vast, infinitely complex game of chess against life itself. In Quebec, I'd found myself backed into a corner. I hadn't been able to see a way out of that situation, and had lost the motivation to find one. Since then, I'd been making small, opportunistic moves, with no clear sense of direction.

The search for May would give me a purpose and direction again. It would give my life meaning once more. If I could find a way to get myself out of that corner, if I could duck and weave my way across the board, I might just be able to get May back in the game.

I had no illusions about how safe or simple it might be, or how much control I'd have over the outcome. It would be a game of bluff, patience, quick thinking, and calculated risks. I'd need both luck and skill. It was extremely likely that I'd never succeed, no matter what I did, and it was very possible that it would end badly for me – but at least I'd go down fighting for something I believed in.

I'd never been much good at chess, but I was determined to give it my best shot. The whole thing seemed crazy, if not impossible – but I was sure it was the right thing to do.

Everyone gives their life for something. They trade their time for possessions, experiences, and connections. Many simply follow the herd, or the path of least resistance – they do what they're told, and collect whatever they find along the way. The path I'd chosen certainly wouldn't be an easy one, but at least it was my own conscious choice.

I remembered the idle fantasy I'd had on that first morning in Sapa, my imagined exhibition of portraits with each picture labelled "Human, Earth". I'd seen those two words as a way of erasing boundaries between people, no matter how distant or different those people might be.

There at Vanessa's house, I took a permanent marker and wrote the words "THE HUMAN, EARTH PROJECT" across a blank piece of paper. I scanned the words onto my laptop, and quickly rearranged them into a bold, simple design.

'The Human, Earth Project' – that was the name of the path I could now feel beneath my feet. That afternoon in southern California, I could never have imagined where that path would lead me, and what an incredible journey it would be.

SILVER COIN

Whatever 'The Human, Earth Project' might become, one thing was certain: I would need some money.

What little I'd saved in Quebec was almost gone, and I couldn't legally work in California. I still had my Canadian working holiday visa, but what could I do?

At home in Australia, I'd studied filmmaking, and had worked as an editor and cameraperson on documentaries and corporate films. I'd won the only filmmaking competition I'd ever entered, for a short documentary on adolescent substance abuse – but that was years ago.

I had no contacts in Canada, and there was a gaping three-year hole in my resume. I didn't have enough money to secure my own place to live, but wouldn't allow myself to rely on the generosity of friends any longer.

The solution, I realised, was to do what so many young Australians had done before me: I began applying for work at ski resorts in the Canadian Rockies.

Almost immediately, I was offered a night security job at Lake Louise, which I readily accepted.

The job would involve long nights walking patrols around the ski resort and nearby staff accommodation. When I received the offer, I still couldn't put any weight on my bruised and swollen foot, and didn't know when I'd be able to walk normally again.

Fortunately, there was plenty of time: the ski season didn't start for another six weeks.

For almost a week, I was so caught up with 'The Human, Earth Project' that I didn't even look at the documents I'd received from Lake Louise. I casually opened the envelope one afternoon and discovered that I was scheduled to start work just two days later, broken foot and all.

I booked a flight immediately, crammed my foot into a boot, thanked Vanessa for her hospitality, and turned north into the coming winter.

DAYSLEEPER

At Lake Louise, I was part of a small security team living and working in "Chucktown" – an enormous log cabin which housed 240 people over the winter season.

Lake Louise shared the same problems as any other ski resort: too much testosterone, and too many illicit substances. When the pot boiled over, the staff began fighting each other, breaking furniture, and acting out wild drunken dares. It was our job to keep order.

It was a strange job for someone who was perpetually underweight, could barely walk, and preferred to avoid violence, but I enjoyed it nonetheless.

Some of the security guards saw their job as enforcing discipline. They wielded power with threats and a macho swagger, and quickly made enemies amongst the other staff.

I saw my job as helping people to stay safe and

comfortable. They came to me with problems, and I helped find the best solutions.

I hobbled through ten-hour shifts, clocking off at 4am. My foot never healed properly, but I began to save a little money, and the long nights gave me time to plan my return to Asia.

Realistically, there was every chance that 'The Human, Earth Project' would fail, and that I would never find May. It was more than a year since she'd been sold. I didn't know where she was, what had happened to her, or even if she was still alive.

If Zao was right, May was somewhere in China – and if she was wrong, May could be anywhere.

I'd begun researching human trafficking, and what I discovered was mind-blowing. I'd understood that it was a huge and horrific problem, but its true scope staggered me.

In China, as in many parts of the world, sons were valued more highly than daughters. It was a son's duty to continue the family line, and to take care of his ageing parents. A daughter, on the other hand, was of little use to her parents. She would essentially be transferred to her husband's family when she married.

Designed to curb population growth, China's notorious "one-child" policy had been enforced since 1980, limiting most families to a single child. With a preference for boys, tens of millions of baby girls were aborted, killed, or abandoned. China was now suffering the aftereffects of this policy, including the world's most extreme gender imbalance.

Many of the boys had now become men, but there just weren't enough women for them to marry. A monstrous vacuum had been created, which was now sucking in girls and young women from neighbouring regions. Its victims were taken from wherever they could be found – including Sapa.

Sapa was just a stone's throw from the border, and it seemed almost certain that May had been forced into marriage or prostitution in China. In either case, she would have been stripped of her clothes, mobile phone, and any identification. It was very possible she'd been given a new name. She would be living essentially as a prisoner in a brothel or private home, controlled by her captors, and dependent on them for her survival.

I could understand these things in an abstract way, but struggled to comprehend the fact that my friend had actually been forced to endure them. My mind refused to grasp it.

How could anyone have looked at that funny, fearless little girl and seen only a dollar value? How could they have been so heartless? What had they done to her, and where was she now?

In all likelihood, May herself didn't even know where she was. After a year in China, she might understand a few words of Chinese, but she wouldn't be able to read at all, and it seemed extremely unlikely that her captors would want to help her.

Even after three decades of the "one-child" policy,

China was still the world's most populous country by far, with almost one-fifth of the world's population. If you counted every single person in the United States, Canada, and every country in Europe, then you added the populations of Australia, New Zealand, and Russia, you'd still need another *hundred million people* to match the number of people in China.

Geographically, it was a huge country – larger than the United States, including Alaska – and May could be anywhere in it, the most insignificant of needles in an incomprehensibly large haystack. It was very likely that she had been sold more than once, and passed along a chain which could stretch across China in any direction.

I'd be venturing into a world of corruption and organised crime. My odds of finding May were infinitesimally small, and my odds of finding trouble were far greater.

Once I was in China, I would be essentially alone, cut off from anyone who might want to provide support. As a highly-conspicuous Westerner, I had no hope of blending in with the locals, and would be the easiest of targets for anyone who wanted to harm me.

As if the odds stacked against me weren't already high enough, I faced language barriers on every side. I didn't speak Hmong, Vietnamese, or Chinese, and didn't know where I might find any interpreters foolhardy enough to follow me where I was going.

I had no idea what the investigation was likely to cost financially. If I reached China only to run out of money, the entire project would be a senseless waste.

I wasn't earning much money in Canada – little more than the minimum wage. It might take me years to save the money I needed, and I simply couldn't wait that long. I'd delayed too long already.

I realised I couldn't do it alone – 'The Human, Earth Project' needed support. But how could I get anyone to support a project which was almost certainly doomed to fail?

MOONLIGHT MILE

In the small hours of the morning, I was patrolling the darkened, log-lined hallways of Chucktown. It was a quiet night, the building was asleep, and my foot was aching. As I sank into a chair in the reception area, I noticed an old magazine left lying on a table nearby – the December 2009 issue of 'Outside' magazine.

The entire issue was focused on "changing the world", featuring articles on various humanitarian and environmental efforts. As I flipped through it, one headline in particular caught my eye: "How to Save the World and Influence People". It was a three-page article written by Pulitzer Prize-winning journalist Nicholas Kristof.

Drawing on research and extensive personal experience, Kristof explained why worthy humanitarian causes so often failed to gain the support they needed. It was all a matter of how the story was presented, he said.

The approach had to be emotional, rather than statistical. Rather than focus on a group or general cause – for example, the Hmong people, or human trafficking – the key was to focus on an individual. Otherwise, people simply became overwhelmed.

I recalled my own experiences picking up garbage in Asia. I'd felt helpless in the face of the larger problem, yet felt empowered by picking up even a single piece of litter. While garbage wasn't a great analogy for human beings, the principle was the same.

When Kristof went on assignment, he would cherry-pick an ideal individual to be the focus of his story. I didn't have that luxury. The focus of 'The Human, Earth Project' was May, and her story had already begun – but maybe I could learn how best to frame May's story, to get the support I needed to help her.

In Kristof's experience, the type of individual whose story resonated best with an audience was a young, spirited female. In that sense, May was perfect – but Kristof's other news was far less encouraging.

The most crucial factor in winning support, he said, was to present "positive, heartwarming accounts of triumph".

Nobody wanted to hear a sad story that would only make them feel hopeless, and May's story was exactly that: hopeless.

Whichever way you looked at it, my chances of finding May were laughably small. There was no way to turn that story into the little ray of sunshine that people wanted in their lives. With a story so bleak, there seemed to be very little hope of getting anyone to listen, and no hope of getting the support I needed.

I had to find another way.

COMMON PEOPLE

I was stuck.

If I was to have any chance of helping May, I needed the support of other people. To get the support of other people, I'd have to find another way to tell May's story – but how?

One of the perks of my security job was living and working in the same building. Between patrols and other duties, I was free to go back to my apartment, so long as I carried my two-way radio and was ready to respond at short notice.

Towards the end of another long night, when Chucktown had at last subsided into silence, I went home and turned on my laptop. I began idly flicking through my photos from Asia again, with only one thought in my mind – *I needed to get more people.*

I'd made a collection of my favourite portraits from

Asia, almost all of which had been taken in impoverished rural villages. I watched the faces flicker slowly past – young and old, male and female.

I needed to get more people.

The idea arrived fully-formed. There were no more doubts or questions in my mind – in an instant, I knew exactly what I would do.

I'd spent three years and three months living and travelling in Asia. It had been an epic overland journey by bus, train, and ferry, tracing a long, circuitous route through eleven countries: Indonesia, Malaysia, Singapore, Thailand, Myanmar (also known as Burma), Laos, Cambodia, Vietnam, China, Nepal, and India.

I'd taken hundreds of portraits along the way. I'd shared a moment with each of those people – but the vast majority of them were strangers to me. With very few exceptions, I didn't know their names, and didn't know where they lived. In fact, I didn't know much about their lives at all – only that their lack of education and resources left them in the demographic most at risk of human trafficking.

I decided to cut my collection down to 99 portraits, and retrace the steps of my original journey to find as many of those people as I could. I'd give each of those people a print of the original portrait I'd taken, and I'd take a new one. I'd listen to their stories, and share them online. It would be an exciting, exotic adventure with plenty of opportunity for "positive, heartwarming accounts of triumph" along the way.

Nestled within that project would be something far darker – my own, seemingly impossible investigation into May's abduction. May's portrait – the one I'd taken by the lake in Sapa – would be the 100th portrait.

The longer journey wasn't going to be easy – in fact, it was going to make the entire project ten times more complicated. It was going to take an incredible investment of time and energy, but if I could use it to bring a little ray of sunshine into people's lives, then I might just get the support I needed to find May.

I didn't sleep at all that night. After my shift ended at 4am, I remained awake, turning the idea over in my mind.

I'd rarely shared any of my portraits before. I began selecting the images and ordering them in such a way that they formed not just a collection of photographs, but an emotional journey in themselves.

We humans have a habit of unconsciously echoing other people's facial expressions. Seeing someone upset makes us feel upset, and seeing someone smile makes us smile. I wanted to make it impossible for anyone to look through my collection of portraits without responding emotionally.

I began the series with some of the more distant, neutral expressions, before transitioning to a select few images that seemed somewhat tense, even confrontational. Then, little by little, I allowed the humour and happiness to shine through, progressing gradually from the subtlest of smiles through great big grins to explosive, unrestrained expressions of joy.

"A celebration of humanity", I dubbed it.

While it would be wonderful to return to Asia, to see all of those people and places again, it certainly wasn't going to be a holiday – it would be a huge amount of hard work. I didn't want to waste time and money when I could be searching for May, and I set myself an ambitious, punishing schedule.

By my conservative estimate, it would be an overland journey of twenty thousand kilometres – half the length of the equator. Most of that distance would be covered by bus, and often on bad roads. It was a journey which had previously taken thirty-nine months – and this time, I'd give myself just six months to complete it.

I'd spend a quarter of that time in Sapa, investigating May's disappearance. If I couldn't find the clues I needed in six weeks, I doubted I ever would.

I now had a positive story – but I didn't know how best to share it, and convert it into the material support I needed.

My elder brother, Nick, had recently arrived in Lake Louise, and was staying with me while he searched for an apartment of his own. In the morning, I told him my idea, and asked his opinion.

Nick suggested crowdfunding. I'd never heard the term before, and he explained it to me. You could share an idea online, he said – and, if people thought it was a good idea, they could send you money to help make it a reality. In return for their support, you could offer them various rewards and incentives.

It sounded almost too good to be true – it was exactly what I needed. I began exploring various crowdfunding websites, and was amazed at what I found. There were projects which seemed absurd to me, yet had succeeded in raising vast amounts of money. Some projects had raised millions of dollars.

I had no intention of profiting from 'The Human, Earth Project', or of taking advantage of anyone's generosity, and I didn't want to ask for any more than seemed necessary.

I sketched out a budget, and decided to ask for $9,325 to make 'The Human, Earth Project' possible. More than half of that money would be used to cover crowdfunding fees, rewards for supporters, travel insurance, tourist visas, a one-way flight to Asia, and photo prints to give to the people I was searching for, if and when I was able to find them again.

The rest of the money – just $25 a day – would cover my living expenses and travel costs. If I needed any more money than that, I would have to earn it myself in Canada before the journey began.

For such an ambitious project, it seemed a modest goal, and – with a little hard work – I was sure I could achieve it. I began preparing all the information and images I'd need.

Nick was the first supporter of my nascent project. He offered to build a website for the project – a website he was to gradually expand and manage for the next two years. Nick also played a supporting role during my later investigations in Vietnam and China.

I needed to record a video for the crowdfunding campaign, but didn't have any video equipment. I borrowed Nick's digital camera, used a stack of books for a tripod, and recorded a simple message in my tiny Chucktown bedroom.

'The Human, Earth Project' was rapidly becoming a reality.

FIRE IT UP

The website, portrait gallery, crowdfunding page, and video were all ready by 12th March, 2013. Without any warning or preamble, I launched them both immediately.

People were surprised by the project, and I was equally surprised by the response. My inbox was immediately flooded with messages of support. They came pouring in from all over the world, gushing with adjectives like "amazing", "inspiring", "brilliant", "beautiful", "exciting", "incredible", "wonderful", and "fantastic". Friends and strangers praised my portraits. One said the project was one of the greatest ideas he'd ever heard; another thanked me for showing her how beautiful humans really were.

Some people knew May personally and – though they might have met her only briefly, or years earlier

– described the deep impression she'd left, and the memories they still held of her. One told me, quite seriously, that May had changed her life. Others said she was one of the loveliest and most memorable locals they'd met in their extensive travels around Asia and the world.

I received prayers and blessings. Many people considered themselves indebted to me, said they'd be honoured to help, and offered their full support. Some recognised the danger and near-impossibility of trying to find May, hailed me as a true hero for trying, and cautioned me to be careful.

"If I can't do it myself," wrote one, "I should at least support a guy with the heart, guts, and brains who can."

A few of the messages were less positive. Some people were doubtful of my intentions and abilities. One friend joked that I'd discovered a new way to pay for my travels. It was a little discouraging, but understandable – my friends knew me as a traveller, not an activist. Even my closest friends in Australia were unaware of what I'd been through in Quebec, and how that experience had changed me.

It's good to be sceptical of anyone who claims to be acting in the best interests of others, and especially those who are raising funds to do so. It was my responsibility to demonstrate the integrity of the project, and the seriousness of my intent.

I also received messages of a more practical nature. I was contacted by Laura, a young Englishwoman who knew May, and had been teaching English in Hanoi when May went missing. Laura had done what I had not: she had returned to Sapa and conducted investigations of her own, shortly after May's disappearance.

While Laura had come no closer to identifying May's kidnappers, she'd acquired a copy of May's birth certificate and further details of the kidnapping, which she passed on to me.

My Hmong friends from Sapa had been able to tell me little beyond the basic fact of May's abduction, and Laura's information was the best I'd yet received.

It seemed there had been an Australian man living in Sapa for three months in early 2011. After returning home, he'd sponsored May to attend school in Hanoi.

According to Laura, May had planned to go to Hanoi around 15th July, with an unidentified female friend who was also enrolled at the school. However, May's father fell ill, and she'd decided to stay at home for a few more days to help the family.

May had disappeared the next day, 16th July 2011, and nobody had heard from her since.

It seemed that May had recently been spending time with a young Hmong man who was said to be attending school in Lao Cai, on the Chinese border. Nobody knew exactly who he was or which village he was from, and he hadn't been seen in Sapa again.

Was this the "Hmong boy" Zao had referred to in her message?

According to May's Hmong friends, it seemed a

young Hmong man had offered May a ride to her village on the back of his motorbike, but had taken her towards the border instead. May's last known contact with anyone in Vietnam had been a final phonecall with her cousin Zao. When May's family and friends tried to call her again, her phone was out of range, or switched off.

May was not the only girl who had disappeared. A Dutch friend I'd met in Sapa had recently returned there, and confirmed what I'd already feared: that May's friend Pang had also been kidnapped, and was also believed to have been sold in China.

I remembered the moody, moon-faced girl I'd often joked with on the street near the Yellow Dragon. It was shocking to think that she'd also been taken. Shadows were seeping through my treasured memories of Sapa, darkening and distorting what had been such a wonderful time in my life.

I was already determined to do everything I could for May. Was I willing to do the same for Pang? Pang and I had never been especially close, and had irritated each other on more than one occasion.

Did that make Pang any less worthy of my attention? Of course not. The project was about doing something decent for humanity. That wasn't limited to one particular individual, or only some people I liked better than others.

It was about doing whatever I could for whoever needed it most – and Pang certainly fit that description.

I remembered Kristof's article, and the importance of focusing a story on a single person. Even just one more person would cause an audience to lose interest, he warned.

The solution was simple. I would do everything I could to help Pang – but I wouldn't mention it publicly. For the sake of winning attention to our cause, Pang would have to remain hidden. My search for Pang would have to be conducted in secret, without any public support.

Of all the messages I received, however, the one that affected me the most was written by a stranger named Michael Brosowski. Michael's message said simply that May had already been returned home safely.

My heart skipped a beat. Could it be true?

Michael was the Australian founder of Blue Dragon Children's Foundation, a Hanoi-based NGO dedicated to helping young people in Vietnam. Over the past decade, Blue Dragon had rescued hundreds of children and young adults who had been trafficked into prostitution, marriage, and forced labour across Vietnam and China.

Had May already been found and rescued? Was my investigation over, even before it had begun?

I wanted to believe Michael's message, but it made no sense to me. I'd been speaking regularly with several of May's friends in Sapa, and they hadn't heard anything from her.

After a brief consultation, Michael and I soon

realised it was a case of mistaken identity. May's legal name wasn't May at all, but Vu. She'd chosen the name May for herself. The rescued girl wasn't May – it was her friend Vu, the skinny little girl who had clung to the fringes of May's group.

I'd been shocked to learn of May's disappearance. Now I realised it wasn't just one friend who had been abducted – at least three of my friends had been taken, in separate incidents. Vu had been rescued, but May and Pang were still missing.

How many more of the Hmong girls I'd known had been kidnapped?

I'd seen the statistics – but they were faceless numbers, and carried no emotional weight for me. Now, for the first time, I began to see the true magnitude of the problem, and how desperately important this work was.

I knew I was on the right path – but where was it leading me?

SHINE A LIGHT

What had happened to May and her friends had not been isolated incidents – far from it.

As I learned more, I realised that Sapa was in the throes of a major human trafficking crisis, which only seemed to be getting worse each year.

The most disturbing realisation was that the abductions had begun even before I'd arrived in Vietnam. I'd been having the time of my life in Sapa, completely oblivious to the fact that girls were being kidnapped from the streets I walked every day.

If I'd been living smack-bang in the middle of a human trafficking crisis and hadn't been aware of it, how was anyone else to know?

Something had to be done – not just for May and her friends, but to help protect the other girls in danger.

The first step in solving any problem is awareness. I

wanted to learn as much as I could about the situation, and share that knowledge with others – but how? And why would people care?

As an English-speaking Westerner, I belonged to a population that was perhaps the most privileged and powerful in history. We, of all people, had the greatest power to change the world – but most people in the Western world had never even heard of Sapa, and few knew who the Hmong people were.

Why would anyone care about a group of impoverished tribespeople living in remote villages on the other side of the world?

Having worked as a filmmaker, my thoughts naturally turned to creating a documentary on the subject. I could use film to transport people to Sapa – to share its sights and sounds, to truly engage them with the place and its people.

As enormous as it was, the human trafficking problem in Sapa was only a tiny part of the global human trafficking story. I couldn't possibly tell the whole story, and it would have been foolish to try. I remembered what Nicholas Kristof had said about focusing on an individual story, rather than overwhelming people with the bigger picture.

I wanted to tell May's story, and use it to help other young women like her.

May's story, up to that point, was a bleak one. I could only hope that it wasn't yet finished, that I could somehow help give her story a more positive ending.

My personal priority was the investigation itself; I'd need someone else to help me film a documentary. I'd have to find a cameraperson who could come with me and record everything. It would have to be a tiny, guerilla-style production – firstly, because there was very little money, and secondly, because we'd have to keep a very low profile.

The investigation, in itself, would already be dangerous enough. We couldn't risk drawing any extra attention to it, from either the traffickers or the authorities. In Sapa, we'd have to pose as tourists and record our interviews in secret, using only the most basic equipment.

I needed someone with a good aesthetic sense, production experience, and preferably their own equipment. They would have to be flexible, familiar with Asia, and unafraid to take risks. It had to be somebody trustworthy, who would be easy to work and travel with. They'd need to commit to a gruelling, six-month journey, and a potentially life-threatening investigation.

I needed someone who could do all this – but I didn't have any money to pay them. The best I could offer was to cover all of their food, accommodation, and travel costs, and give them an equal share in the documentary itself. In reality, I didn't know if I could afford even that much.

Fortunately, I knew just the right person, and I hoped that he'd be interested.

In 2009, before my arrival in Vietnam, I'd been

living in southern Thailand, where I'd shared a house with a Frenchman named Patrice. Patrice had been living a double life, splitting his time between his work at a renowned restaurant in Paris and his passion for travel photography, which he indulged in Africa and Southeast Asia.

At that time, Patrice and I both faced the same dilemma: whether or not to invest in serious photographic equipment and turn professional. I chose not to, and had since given up photography entirely. Patrice, on the other hand, had taken the leap, and had been working as a travel photographer ever since. His images had been widely published and exhibited, and he'd even received a prize from world-renowned photographer Yann Arthus-Bertrand.

While he was primarily a photographer, Patrice also shot video, and his work was excellent. He was a fearless cameraman who had worked on the front lines during the 2010 Red Shirt riots in Bangkok.

Patrice and I discussed the project, the route, and the timing. I was in luck – our plans dovetailed neatly, and Patrice agreed to join me as a cameraperson.

The project was no longer a "me", but an "us".

Meanwhile, I received an unexpected message.

Marinho was another European I'd met in Asia, in 2011. We didn't really know each other at all – we'd met only once, and briefly, while queueing for tickets at a train station in Delhi. Marinho was a tanned, broad-shouldered academic. He wore glasses and a goatee, and had an intellectual, almost revolutionary, air about him.

After a brief but interesting conversation, Marinho and I had gone our separate ways. We'd connected on social media, and had barely spoken since.

When I shared my project, including the portrait gallery, Marinho messaged me, wanting to know if there was some way to share his own photography through the project.

It was an unusual question, and piqued my curiosity. I asked to see his photography, and was impressed by what I saw.

Marinho came from a family of photographers. He wanted to travel and take more pictures, but he was stuck at home in Europe, in a job that paid very little.

Although he was little more than a stranger and had very little experience with filmmaking, I knew it would be a lot easier to produce the documentary if we had a third crew member, and it seemed like a good opportunity for all three of us.

I couldn't afford it – but then, I couldn't really afford Patrice, either. As with so many other aspects of the project, it was a gamble, based on a gut decision.

After speaking to Patrice, I offered Marinho a position on the team, and he accepted. The three of us would produce the documentary together, as partners. I would take responsibility for all travel costs, though I had no idea how I was going to pay for it.

Just as I didn't really know Marinho, he didn't really know me. He was also taking a gamble, leaving his work and home for a project which seemed shaky at best. Marinho had his own share of doubts and questions, and there was little I could say to reassure him.

When he asked what we'd need to produce the documentary, I sent him a list of equipment: cameras, microphones, tripods, storage media, and a powerful laptop with specialised software.

"I currently have none of these things," I concluded.

Marinho wanted to know what the plan was when we reached Sapa, but I really didn't know.

"We'll do what we can," I said.

BUSY EARNIN'

'The Human, Earth Project' was an accurate reflection of that moment in my life. Founded on ideals, rather than practicalities, it was fuelled by willpower and very little else.

One thing I'd learned in my travels around the world is what a difference it could make to speak to people in their own language. By making a little extra effort, you could transform the experience completely, for everyone involved.

I thought it would be great to have our website translated into two or three foreign languages, to broaden its appeal. As I was chatting with a friend about the Spanish translation, she casually mentioned that she'd be happy to provide Portuguese and Greek translations, too.

Why not? I thought.

And then I thought: Why stop there?

I had friends all over the world who loved the idea of the project, and were enthusiastic to lend a hand. I realised it would be especially useful to have translations made in the languages of the Asian countries we'd be travelling through. When Patrice, Marinho, and I began our journey, it would be wonderful to be able to explain our work to the local people in their own tongue.

Of course, I had no idea how incredibly complicated or time-consuming this would be for myself and my brother Nick, who was running the website.

After chatting with some of my friends around the world, I messaged Nick to say we might end up having the website translated into twenty or even thirty languages.

"What?" he said. "There aren't even that many. You got it in Klingon or something?"

I'd soon organised translations into Afrikaans, Arabic, Chinese (both Simplified and Traditional), Czech, Dutch, Finnish, French, German, Greek, Hebrew, Hindi, Hmong, Indonesian, Italian, Japanese, Khmer, Korean, Malaysian, Nepali, Norwegian, Persian, Portuguese, Punjabi, Russian, Spanish, Swedish, and Vietnamese.

Twenty-nine languages: for a such a tiny project with such a tight budget, I'm sure it must have been a world first. All of those translations were given freely, by people who wanted to see the project succeed.

In a way, this was just what I'd hoped the project

would do – bring people together, regardless of their background, and give them a chance to make a positive difference in the world. It was incredible to see it actually happening.

It was also utterly impractical, of course. Difficulties with foreign character sets meant that some of the languages never worked properly – and then we had to take all of the translations down five months later, when we rewrote everything on the website.

Nick was extremely patient about the whole episode.

That experience had been harmless enough – but practicalities soon began intruding on the project in other, more painful ways.

It was the first time I'd run a fundraising campaign, and it wasn't nearly as simple as I'd imagined. I knew little about social media, and less about fundraising.

I'd shared the project with my friends and May's, and almost everyone who saw it was enthusiastic about it. Dozens of people contributed, and many people shared the project with their own friends – then it lost momentum, and I didn't know what else to do.

I was beginning to learn one of the hardest lessons of fundraising: getting moral support is easy, but it doesn't necessarily translate to financial support.

Numerous people wrote to tell me of their intention to contribute. Some even told me exactly when and how much they planned to give. Two people said they'd organise their own local fundraiser to ensure I received the funds I needed.

Some of those people followed through. Most simply disappeared.

It was another reminder of the importance of action, and how little intention ultimately mattered. I didn't blame those people, but I wouldn't allow myself to become one of them. I was determined to follow through on the commitments I'd made, regardless of how difficult that might be.

The trouble was, I'd made a lot of commitments.

I'd seen the crowdfunding campaign as a compromise. I would make the far longer and more difficult journey to find the other 99 people I'd photographed, if it helped me get the funds I needed to search for May.

That plan had backfired spectacularly. I'd succeeded in raising only three thousand dollars – less than a third of my goal. In doing so, I'd made commitments that would cost much more than that, and delay my return to Vietnam by several months.

In my determination to share May's story as a documentary, I'd made my situation far more complicated.

I now needed to pay six months' worth of food, accommodation, and travel expenses for not one but three people. I had to buy three times as many visas, three travel insurance policies, and two return flights from Europe to Asia, in addition to my own flight from North America.

I'd have to buy two sets of cameras and lenses (for Marinho and myself), plus microphones, tripods, storage devices, batteries, and carry cases.

There would be extra expenses involved in the search for Pang, too, though I couldn't guess how much they might be.

I estimated the project would cost around thirty thousand dollars, at a bare minimum – and I'd raised only a tenth of that. I'd have to spend far more than three thousand dollars before I even reached Asia.

Borrowing money wasn't an option. It wasn't a commercial project, and there was no guarantee that the documentary would ever break even, let alone turn a profit. It made no sense to take on so much debt, even if I could convince someone to loan me the money.

I began frantically writing letters for sponsorship – but again, I didn't know what I was doing. I received few responses and no serious interest, much less any support.

It would have made more sense to cancel the rest of the journey, and go directly back to Vietnam to begin the search for May – but I couldn't let myself do that. I'd made promises, and the project was now tied to my own reputation as a trustworthy human being. Dozens of people around the world had put their faith in me, and I wasn't going to let them down.

Fortunately, I'd allowed myself a little extra time. My first journey through Asia had begun in Indonesia on 10th September 2008. Patrice, Marinho, and I were scheduled to begin our journey in the same place, exactly five years later, on 10th September 2013.

I stayed in Lake Louise for the summer, and worked like a madman. I took on extra shifts, then extra jobs. I made beds, cleaned toilets, and painted cabins. I worked behind the counter at the staff grocery store. Some weeks I worked over a hundred hours, and barely slept. I'd come home from a full day's work, change one uniform for another, and go straight onto a ten-hour nightshift with the security team. After clocking off at 4am, I'd catch three hours' sleep, and start again at 8am.

Whatever I did, I knew it would never be enough. The project was going to run out of money – that was inevitable. The only question was how far we could get before that happened.

MESSAGES

A month before I left Lake Louise, I went rockclimbing with a friend on the cliffs behind the lake.

At the base of one of the more difficult climbs, I saw a slender Asian man standing atop a small stone slab. He wasn't even looking at the wall of rock that towered over him; he didn't have to. As I watched, he began practicing the motions of the climb.

He reached for invisible folds and wrinkles in the air, crimped his fingers around them, and pulled his body towards them. His torso twisted one way, his leg swung the other. He bent, and flexed. With his eyes closed, and without moving from his perch, the man performed a full-body rehearsal of the entire climb.

When he was ready, he stepped down from the slab, clipped onto the rope, and executed the single most impressive climb I'd ever seen. He was fluid, flowing. At no point did he hesitate, or fumble for a handhold. The holds he needed appeared when he stretched his fingers towards them. He swam, vertically, up the rock face.

The journey that lay ahead of me was a daunting one. Once it began, it wouldn't stop for six relentless months. If I stared up at the wall that towered over me – a wall spanning tens of thousands of kilometres – it seemed like an impossible feat.

But if I closed my eyes, I could picture each of those faces, each village, and each dusty bus ride. I could see myself moving between them, from one to the next, as I counted to one hundred. I felt ready – and I knew that, whatever happened next, it was going to be the journey of a lifetime.

Then I received two surprising messages.

The first came from an Indian-Norwegian man named Frode, whom I knew as a friend of May's, and as a passionate supporter of my project.

Frode was on holiday, and had returned to Sapa for a week. He'd asked several of May's friends about her abduction, and one girl had given him some very interesting news.

May's phone number had stopped working the evening she'd disappeared, almost two years earlier: but May's friend said she'd tried calling the number recently, and it had worked. The phone had been answered by a man who spoke a language she didn't understand – she believed it was Chinese. She had hung up.

The story gave us a straw of hope to cling to. It wasn't

much, but it was all we had, and I struggled to make sense of it. Why would a Chinese-speaking man be using May's phone number?

It was a mystery that May's phone number worked at all. It was possible that, after almost two years of inactivity, the service provider had resold her number, and the man who answered the phone had nothing to do with her trafficking. He might have been a Chinese-speaking resident of Vietnam, or perhaps the language wasn't Chinese at all.

May had almost certainly been stripped of her phone in the first hours after her abduction, somewhere in the border region. It was likely that May's traffickers had kept her phone, and while it would have been foolish to keep the SIM card that linked them to their crime, it was still a possibility.

It was also possible that the phone, and SIM card, had been resold to someone else in the border region – someone who was unconnected to the crime, but who might be able to identify May's traffickers.

At the far end of the spectrum of possibilities, there was a chance that May's phone had remained with her all the way to her final destination, and the man who had answered the phone was there with her. That would be almost too much to hope for, but it had to be considered.

I had to learn more, so that I could begin to eliminate possibilities.

May's number was Vietnamese. I doubted it would

work in China, or if May's friend could have reached it there without entering an international dialling code. It seemed more likely that the phone was still in Vietnam – or in the immediate border region, within reach of Vietnam's signal towers.

I'd heard that many of the trafficked girls were kept just across the border, very close to Vietnam. Perhaps May was much closer to home than I'd imagined.

The year before, while cycling across Spain, I'd met another cyclist named Qiuda. A well-educated young man from Beijing who spoke excellent English and Spanish, Qiuda and I had cycled together until our paths had diverged. We'd remained in contact, and Qiuda had become an ardent supporter of my project.

I discussed Frode's message with Qiuda. The first priority was to discover the phone's location, but it didn't seem possible to track the number through its Vietnamese service provider.

And of course, we couldn't simply call a stranger and ask him where he lived – especially not on a trafficked girl's phone number.

...Or could we?

If Qiuda and I could find a plausible pretext for calling the man, perhaps we could trick him into revealing his location – but we'd only have one chance. While Qiuda was nervous of making a mistake and losing the trail, he was willing to make the call.

We began brainstorming ideas and, gradually, we prepared a plan. Qiuda would call the number, identify himself as a representative of a particular organisation, and ask the man to participate in a two-minute phone survey. As an incentive, Qiuda would offer the man a gift. It had to be something big enough to tempt him, but not so big he'd become suspicious. A gift voucher seemed like the best idea.

Qiuda would then ask the man a series of ten quick and easy questions about his spending habits – nothing that would arouse his suspicion, but just enough to justify the gift. At the end of the questionnaire, Qiuda would ask for a delivery address for the gift voucher.

If Qiuda succeeded in obtaining an address – in Vietnam or China – I would go there and investigate.

It wasn't a perfect plan by any means. Even if it worked, there was only a slender chance that the information could lead us to May – but it was the only hope we had.

After talking through all of the possibilities, Qiuda was ready to make the call. I waited nervously while the minutes ticked away, and at last I received his message – the number didn't work.

Our preparations had all been in vain.

I realised there was a very real possibility that Frode, Qiuda, and I had all overlooked: that May's friend had simply told Frode what he wanted to hear.

As I was soon to discover, it could be incredibly difficult to uncover the truth in Sapa, and this episode was the first hint of how complex and challenging my investigation was to become.

The second surprising message I received that month was more conclusive. It came from Patrice, in Paris.

Patrice's father had suffered a stroke in Marseilles, and was in a critical condition. Patrice was on his way there to be with him. Patrice didn't know when he'd next be able to leave France, and wouldn't be able to join me in Asia.

It was an unexpected blow to the project. Though it eased a little of my financial burden, the documentary would still cost far more than I could afford – and its production was now largely in the hands of Marinho, who was little more than a stranger to me.

But there was no turning back now.

BLINKING LIGHTS (FOR YOU)

Between my long, sleep-deprived summer and the crushing pressure of the journey to come, I'd decided to give myself a week off and return to Burning Man. It was a time I'd set aside for myself to relax and re-energise, though it didn't quite turn out that way.

I'd been receiving regular email updates from the Burning Man organisers all year. Four months before the festival, one of the emails mentioned that Burning Man would be hosting a TEDx event that year, and included an invitation for applications.

At the time, I'd been inundated with messages, and hadn't read the email until two hours before applications were due. It was a fantastic opportunity to share my message on the TEDx stage, and I kicked myself for not having seen the notification earlier.

The form requested quite a lot of detail about

proposed TEDx talks. I'd been busy with my security duties that evening, but managed to find a few minutes to make a rushed, last-minute application. When I didn't hear back from the TEDx organisers, I assumed that my hurried application had been rejected.

My final weeks in Canada were a frantic blur. I was busy packing up my life at Lake Louise, making my preparations for the long journey ahead, and getting ready to spend a week in the desert in between.

In the middle of everything, just a few days before I left Lake Louise, I received notification that my TEDx application had been successful.

It was exciting news – but I had no time to write a speech. I barely had time to sleep.

Worse, I hadn't kept a copy of my application, and couldn't remember what I'd written on it. It hardly seemed appropriate to ask the organisers what I'd promised to speak about.

In late August, I left my apartment and an enjoyable full-time job in the stunningly beautiful Canadian Rockies, which had been my home for the past ten and a half months. I took with me the last paycheck I was to receive for a very, very long time. I said goodbye to my brother Nick, not knowing how many years it would be until I saw him again.

This time, my travel arrangements to Burning Man were far more modest. I took a bus to Vancouver, and an overnight train to Los Angeles. Vanessa and I drove up to Black Rock City in her four-wheel drive, and I slept in a dusty tent. Throughout the journey, I was busy scribbling notes for a speech.

It was Monday when Vanessa and I arrived at Burning Man, and the TEDx event was scheduled for Thursday afternoon. It was going to be a great opportunity to tell May's story and my own, and I wanted to do it properly.

A few months earlier, I'd been contacted by a journalist from CBC, Canada's national broadcasting network. She thought my project would make a wonderful story, and had convinced her TV crew to make the two-hour journey from Calgary to interview me for a segment on the evening news.

I'd been incredibly nervous, and had given a terrible interview. I felt as though I'd wasted the reporter's time, and wasted a fantastic chance to share May's story. This time, I was determined to get it right.

For the first three days of Burning Man, I was like the boy who had to stay back and do his homework while all the other children were out to play.

Our camp was a ramshackle arrangement of couches, chairs, and tables, surrounded by dusty tents and vehicles, and covered by shadecloths. All kinds of strange human beings would stagger into the camp – drunk, drugged, hungover, or only half-awake. Some wore elaborate costumes, while others were practically naked. Those people were my test audience: I'd sit them down, and ask for feedback on my evolving speech.

The TEDx organisers had scheduled two rehearsals before the event, both of which were cancelled at the last moment. Nobody involved in the event had heard my talk at all.

On the day of the event, I practised the speech to a six-metre-tall rubber ducky outside the venue. I was still nervous – especially as I'd been given a strict twelve-minute time limit, and had barely been able to condense my speech to that length.

The venue – a large geodesic dome – was crammed to capacity. Sections of the wall had been removed, and hundreds more were braving the fierce desert sun to listen in from outside. Just moments before I stepped onstage, one of the organisers took me aside.

"We're running ahead of schedule," he said. "Take as long as you like."

The pressure was lifted, the crowd was wonderfully receptive, and the speech went well. Afterwards, when the speech was shared online, it quickly became the most popular of the twelve speeches given that day.

(As new facts emerged over the following months and my understanding of the situation evolved, however, a few of the details I'd shared in my speech ultimately proved untrue.)

I stepped offstage, someone handed me a margarita, and I finally had the time to unwind I'd been hoping for.

On the edge of the chaotic, city-sized party that is Burning Man stands a small refuge of silence and serenity: the Temple.

The Temple, which takes a different form each year,

is the emotional focal point of the festival. For seven days and nights, the temple is filled with prayer and meditation, weddings and memorial services. The walls are scrawled with raw, heartfelt messages of love, loss, and healing.

On the penultimate night of the festival, at the centre of a wild celebration, the Man burns. On the final night, in a much more subdued and emotionally-charged atmosphere, the temple is razed to the ground.

The previous year, the Temple had been an incredibly intricate creation, rising to a tall spire reminiscent of a Burmese pagoda.

This year, the Temple was a great wooden pyramid, its faces constructed in bold geometric patterns. On the stone altar at its core, I placed a photograph of May, with the simple handwritten message:

"Until we meet again."

As the Temple was swallowed by flames, I wondered if there was any real chance of ever seeing May again.

I didn't know – but if there was, I intended to take it.

HANDLE WITH CARE

After the Temple burned, Vanessa and I drove all
night, arriving back at her house the following morning.

There was little time to sleep. I had only one week
until Marinho and I were scheduled to begin filming in
Asia, and we still didn't have any equipment.

I hadn't owned a functional camera since giving up
photography on my first trip to Nepal, nearly three years
earlier, and Marinho's camera had no video capability.

I'd spent months trying to find the right camera-
and-lens combinations for the right price. If I spent too
much money now, Marinho and I might not even reach
Sapa.

Marinho was aware that we were on a tight budget,
but I hadn't told him the full extent of my financial
troubles. I was still hoping for a miracle before the
money ran out.

I'd finally found the equipment we needed for a price I could afford: two Canon 70D camera bodies with basic mid-range zoom lenses for a total of three thousand dollars. They weren't the best cameras on the market – nowhere near it – but they would do the job. Marinho, who would be the principal camera operator, would bring his own tripod and extra lenses from Europe.

I wanted to inspect the cameras before I bought them – but they didn't seem to be available anywhere. After double-checking the details, I realised the cameras were a brand new product, and were to begin shipping only that week.

From Vanessa's house, I contacted several stores in Los Angeles. Nobody had the cameras yet, and couldn't say exactly when they might arrive.

If I ordered two and had them delivered to Vanessa's house, would they arrive before my flight? Or would I arrive in Asia empty-handed, with no equipment to begin filming, and no money to buy replacements?

It was a gamble, but I decided to take it.

The day before my flight, a four-thousand-dollar box full of packing peanuts, camera bodies, lenses, filters, batteries, microphones, and a tripod was delivered to Vanessa's house.

There was no time to familiarise myself with the equipment: I'd have to learn whatever I could along the way.

I had a strange sense of *déjà vu* as I packed my backpack, thanked Vanessa, and rode down to LAX once more – yet I knew that whatever lay ahead would be unlike anything I'd ever before experienced.

The past few months had been one of the most intense times of my life, and my journey had barely begun.

RUNNING ON EMPTY

Marinho and I hit the ground running. From the moment we arrived in Indonesia, we barely had time to breathe. Over the next three months, we travelled ten thousand kilometres by bus, train, ferry, foot, and motorbike, tracing a jagged path across Indonesia, Malaysia, Thailand, and Myanmar.

Marinho and I averaged more than a hundred kilometres of travel per day – a distance that might only be an hour's drive in the West, but could often take far longer in Asia, where nothing was quite as simple as it seemed.

Each day, we had to organise accommodation, food, and transport. We needed guides, and interpreters. I spent my time hunting for clues to help us find each of the 100 people we were looking for – poring over maps, sorting through old photos, trying to decipher notes I'd scribbled in my guidebook five years earlier.

Our search was highly unpredictable and endlessly surprising, and could lead us any distance in any direction.

In one case, we located a man in an entirely different country, several months and many thousands of kilometres from where we'd first begun looking for him. In another, the young woman found me before we'd even begun searching for her. Sometimes, Marinho and I spent days chasing rumours and wildly conflicting stories between scattered villages, and still never found the people we were seeking.

There were countless hours spent organising and sifting through our rapidly-accumulating masses of videos and photographs. There were videos to be edited, photos to be tweaked, animations and graphics to be created, dozens of blog posts to be written, and social media to be managed.

Even when I had the time, I could barely sleep. I was constantly turning over in my mind the endless lists of things that still needed to be done.

We met wonderful people, and heard plenty of incredible stories. Since I'd seen him last, one of the men I was searching for had been tricked into slavery on a palm oil plantation – Marinho and I were with his wife and daughter in their village when he arrived home for the first time in three years. Another person had recently emerged from a 25-day coma. A third had become the head priest of his region just days before our arrival, and performed a special ceremony for our benefit.

And that was just the first two weeks.

When I'd first announced the project, I'd received a sceptical message claiming I'd never find more than 27 of the 100 people I was searching for. Marinho and I quickly passed that number. By the time we returned from Myanmar to Thailand in early December, we'd already found 46 of those people – and we were only halfway through the journey.

Our success, however, had come at a price. Marinho and I had been forced to deal with illness, injury, language barriers, misinformation, and the threat of murder and violence. We'd come face-to-face with a suspected trafficker in Indonesia, become entangled with the military in Myanmar, and I'd almost lost an eye to an exploding firecracker in Thailand.

The journey had been a race against the clock and our rapidly-expiring visas. We'd been roasted by the sun, drenched by monsoonal rains, and bathed in dust. Much of our equipment had been lost, damaged, or destroyed.

And, with every step of the way, our very limited funds were vanishing. Marinho and I saved money wherever we could – we'd cut each other's hair, and wash our clothing in the sink – but we couldn't stop the inevitable.

My final hope of raising the funds I needed to find May was to build up our audience. If we could get enough people engaged and excited about our work, if we could show them we were working hard and making the most of every dollar we received, I thought they'd be more inclined to support us when we really needed it.

It wasn't really a plan so much as an idea, and a vague one at that, but it was all I had.

A marketing expert had seen the project in its first months and said, with such a strong concept, it should have already been ten times larger than it was. It could easily be done, they said – but they were already committed to other projects, I couldn't afford to pay for marketing, and I didn't know how to do it by myself.

We had incredible stories, but I had no talent for social media, and was never able to build the audience we needed.

We had a highly-dedicated audience – but it remained small. Marinho and I were rapidly spending what little money we did have, and our time was running out. It was only a matter of time before the entire project would fall flat on its face.

I felt incredibly frustrated with myself for having promised so much more than I could afford to deliver. I was impatient to arrive in northern Vietnam to begin the search for May – but Marinho and I were both exhausted, and we needed time to rest.

We decided to stop briefly in Chiang Mai, the largest city in northern Thailand, before crossing the border into Laos. What was to be a momentary pause became a full month, and led us in some very unexpected directions.

PEOPLE GET READY

'The Human, Earth Project' was my first experience writing a blog – in fact, I'd never even followed one before. Before I launched the project, in preparation to start writing the blog, I'd begun reading several.

One of the blogs I chanced upon was written by an Irishman named Niall. Several months earlier, I'd reached out and told Niall I enjoyed his writing, and we'd stayed in touch.

Niall and I realised we'd be crossing paths in Chiang Mai, and decided to meet in a café there. Niall brought a Canadian friend, another digital nomad named John.

When he heard about my work, John was fascinated, and wanted to help in some way. He asked me what I needed.

What I desperately needed was money – but I'd barely met John, and wasn't going to say so. Not even

Marinho knew what a terrible financial situation I was in, though I knew I'd have to tell him soon. Until the crunch came, I considered it my own problem, and I brushed John's question aside.

"I just need more time," I said.

John wasn't to be put off so easily, and I hadn't yet realised what a determined person he could be.

If John had told me he was going to raise money for the project, I wouldn't have believed him. Others had said the same thing, and simply disappeared.

But he didn't tell me – he just went ahead and started making plans. Almost before I knew what was happening, John and his friend Barry had assembled a small but dedicated group of digital nomads to brainstorm ideas for my project. They saw my first, failed fundraising campaign, and decided to launch a second campaign on my behalf.

Having learned the true value of action, I had immense respect for John, Barry, and the team they'd assembled. Each of them gave what they could, asking nothing in return. One member of that team – Dustin, from Saskatoon – remains closely involved with the project even now, six years later.

John and Barry called in favours from their extensive contacts in the blogging world, encouraging them all to support the campaign. We soon had over forty bloggers around the world – some of them highly influential – who were ready to spread the word.

The problem was the timing. It was mid-December

when the decision was made to launch a second fundraising campaign. We wanted to prepare and launch the campaign as quickly as possible, while the core team was still together in Chiang Mai – but there was a huge amount of work to be done. Even with such a large team, we wouldn't be able to launch until after Christmas, which was the absolute worst time of year to fundraise.

Initially, we made the unusual and highly ambitious decision to launch the campaign on Boxing Day. When it proved impossible to coordinate so many people over the holiday period, we delayed the launch for another month, until late January.

In the meantime, I was looking ahead to our investigation in Sapa, and the dangers it would involve. Since announcing my intention to search for May, I'd found myself exposed to all kinds of rumours. I struggled to separate fact from fiction, to get a clear sense of the risks Marinho and I would be taking.

I heard a rumour of a Belgian couple who had been imprisoned by the local authorities in Sapa for asking too many questions about human trafficking there.

It seemed that it wasn't just local girls who were disappearing, either: I was told that three foreigners had vanished from the region in the past year alone. They hadn't been found, and it seemed unlikely they would ever be. It was clear that there were ruthless criminal networks operating in Vietnam's northern mountains.

Chiang Mai was a hub not only for digital nomads,

but also for local and international organisations fighting human trafficking. There were many similarities between the trafficking situation in northern Thailand and that of northern Vietnam, with an emphasis on girls and young women from remote ethnic groups being targeted for sex trafficking.

Marinho and I had first begun meeting with counter-trafficking organisations three months earlier in Indonesia. Now we spent more time speaking with various organisations, learning all we could.

It wasn't just a matter of facts and figures: we were preparing to enter the world of human trafficking, where some tiny sliver of information could potentially mean the difference between life and death, or yield a valuable clue to help me find my friends.

In a world where so many people were competing for attention on social media, I'd never had any desire to be in the public eye.

At the same time, I understood that my friendship with May, Pang, and Vu was a key element of the story we were telling to raise awareness of human trafficking. I found myself torn between wanting to inspire a difference in others, and wanting to maintain my privacy.

John and Barry had already decided that my story should be central to our second fundraising campaign – and, when Marinho and I reached Vietnam, I realised that I'd have to appear on camera for the documentary.

I'd never been particularly concerned with my

appearance. As a long-term traveller, I chose my clothes for practicality, and rarely bothered with my hair at all. I usually kept it cut short so I wouldn't have to worry about it.

After three months of hard travelling, my clothes were a mess. I knew I'd have to make myself more presentable, and my family had sent me a little money for Christmas – but I loathed shopping, and shopping centres were some of my least favourite places on Earth.

At Christmas, I finally mustered the resolve to step inside one of Chiang Mai's monstrous shopping centres. Bombarded by advertising and sickened by consumerism, I lost my nerve almost immediately, before I'd even entered any of the shops.

There was a mannequin standing outside the first shop dressed in a black denim jacket and dark green cargo pants. I called the attendant, bought the clothing straight off the mannequin, and fled.

I found a grey-green beanie at the local markets. That completed the outfit I wore over the next year – whenever I appeared on camera, and often when I didn't.

On Boxing Day, Marinho and I organised a human trafficking information evening in Chiang Mai. We invited experts from counter-trafficking organisations to speak about their experiences, and opened the doors to the general public. It was at a wonderful venue with a capacity crowd of tourists, locals, and digital nomads, including our own crowdfunding team.

It had been only fifteen months since I'd begun

researching human trafficking, and I now found myself speaking alongside experts. I recounted the story of the girl who'd fallen in the middle of the road, less than two hundred kilometres from where I was standing. Looking out at the audience, I remembered how little I'd understood of human trafficking, and realised how much my life had changed since then.

I saw how hungry people were for more information once they began to grasp the immensity of the crisis, and I was reminded of the importance of our work.

It was the last time Marinho and I met with John and Barry's fundraising team. Two days later we resumed the journey that was drawing us ever closer to Sapa, and the strange discoveries that awaited us there.

CONTACT

Marinho and I crossed the Mekong River into Laos. Among the minority villages scattered along the northern border, we found five more of the 100 people we were searching for. We welcomed the new year with a Hmong family in Muang Sing, just three hundred kilometres from Sapa.

It had been over two years since I'd received Zao's message telling me of May's abduction. I'd followed a long, strange path since that day – through denial and despair, disorientation and determination, as I'd travelled around the world and back again.

It would have been so much simpler if I'd gone straight back to Sapa as soon as I'd heard about May's abduction, I thought. Then I remembered May's friend Laura, who had done exactly that, and had come no closer to finding May. I'd been waiting for so long to get back to Sapa – but what would I do there? What could I possibly do that Laura hadn't already done?

In the past two years, nothing had changed. The trail was stone cold, and I knew that there was no real hope of ever finding May.

Now, my path was leading me away from Sapa once more. Rather than crossing directly to Vietnam, Marinho and I would take a far longer route. We'd follow the Mekong River south, to search for three more people I'd photographed in Cambodia, before making the long journey back up the Vietnamese coast and into the northern mountains.

It was a detour of four thousand kilometres, and several weeks – but it no longer seemed to make any difference. I could begin my investigation now, next month, or even next year, and the outcome would be the same. I knew I'd never find May: there were just too many pieces missing from the puzzle.

Barry had also left Chiang Mai, and was now housesitting in the Laotian capital, Vientiane. Marinho and I turned south and stayed with Barry for a few days, while we worked together on the upcoming fundraising campaign.

I'd often chat with my Hmong and Kinh friends from Sapa. Each time I asked if there was any news about May, the response was always the same: nobody knew where May was, or what had happened to her.

On 8th January I was chatting with one of May's cousins, a girl named Ha. As ever, I asked about May

– and, as ever, there was no news.

Less than an hour later, Ha messaged me again, saying: "One of my friend just send me an email and she said that she hear from May. May got marry and she has a baby".

I was staggered.

For the first time since her abduction, May had succeeded in making contact with someone in Sapa, and the news sounded hopeful. It seemed as if May had been forced into marriage, rather than prostitution – but where was she? Was she okay? Did she want to come home?

I needed to know how May had made contact. If she had called, which number had she called from?

Getting that phone number was crucial. If I could get that number, then – for the first time in almost two and a half years – we could contact May. There would be a real chance of helping her, and perhaps even of bringing her home to her family in Vietnam.

Ha didn't have any further information. She said she'd received the news from a girl named Yau.

I didn't know anyone named Yau. Ha gave me Yau's contact details, and I was surprised to discover that this mysterious stranger was in fact my friend, and May's cousin, Zao.

Not only did Zao have the phone number May had used to call home from China, she also had a contact number for Pang in China. Pang, too, had recently made contact for the first time; I was told that she was also now married in China, and had two babies.

It was incredible news. I was stunned that Zao hadn't told me earlier, but there was no time for such questions.

I hadn't even reached Sapa yet, and my investigation had already gone further than I could have reasonably hoped. I immediately cancelled all other plans – Marinho and I had to get to Vietnam as quickly as possible.

First of all, we'd need Vietnamese visas. There was a Vietnamese embassy just a few kilometres away in central Vientiane, and I realised it was closing in less than an hour. If we hurried, Marinho and I could still get there in time to make our applications that morning.

There was a battered old motorbike at the house where Barry was housesitting, and he said we could take it. Marinho offered to drive. We grabbed our passports, jumped on the bike, and sped off towards the city centre – but we never reached the embassy.

I can't remember now if we were speeding or if we'd run a red light (quite possibly both), but we were pulled over by the police within the first few blocks.

Somehow, Marinho talked his way out of it, and we rode away – only to be caught by a larger group of policemen on the very next block. This time, they'd caught us making an illegal U-turn, and they were taking the matter much more seriously. They chastised Marinho for not wearing a helmet and, when they checked our motorbike's registration, discovered we had none. Vietnam suddenly seemed very far away.

To my amazement, Marinho talked his way out of

trouble for the second time in twenty minutes. Again, the police let him ride away – with no helmet, and no registration – but we'd lost valuable time. There was no hope of reaching the embassy in time, so we turned back.

With a weekend approaching, I realised we could get our visas more quickly in Luang Prabang, two hundred kilometres to the north. Marinho and I said goodbye to Barry, boarded an overnight bus to Luang Prabang, and – visas in hand – took another bus to Hanoi the very next evening.

It was a long, exhausting journey from Luang Prabang to Hanoi: over twenty-four hours along twisted, broken roads through the mountainous borderlands. The bus departed in the evening and arrived late the following night.

Marinho and I arrived in Hanoi hungry, sleep-deprived, and utterly spent – and our real work was just beginning.

HEROES

Hanoi was a chaotic, crowded city of seven million people on the banks of the Red River. Punctured by lakes and temples, choked with clouds of grey smog, its streets surged with endless torrents of cars and snarling motorbikes.

The city was home to Blue Dragon Children's Foundation and its founder, Michael Brosowski. It had been almost ten months since I'd received that first startling message from Michael, telling me that May had already been returned home. He and I had remained in contact, and now – for the first time – we had an opportunity to meet in person.

We arranged a rendezvous at Blue Dragon's headquarters. For security reasons, it was an unmarked building discreetly hidden behind a tall, plain fence in central Hanoi.

Michael greeted Marinho and me at the gate, and led us upstairs. Lean and well-spoken, in his late thirties, he was to become my advisor through the difficult and dangerous months ahead.

With a childhood split between Sydney and rural New South Wales, Michael had first arrived in Hanoi as an English teacher twelve years earlier. His volunteer work with street children had led him ever-deeper into the shadowy world of human trafficking, and I couldn't have asked for a better guide to that world. When he spoke of the trade in human lives, Michael spoke with intelligence, empathy, and deep understanding.

Blue Dragon was fighting human trafficking on all fronts, with programs focused on awareness, prevention, rescue, and aftercare. Their staff of over sixty people included social workers, psychologists, lawyers, and teachers. Over the years, Blue Dragon had gradually expanded their operations from Hanoi up into the northern mountains, and down into central Vietnam. Theirs was the only organisation in Vietnam rescuing trafficked girls from China.

Michael was generous with his time and experience. He spent the entire morning and part of the afternoon with me, discussing the Vietnamese trafficking situation in general, and May and Pang's cases in particular.

My interest wasn't merely academic – Michael was spelling out the rules of the game on which Marinho and I would soon be gambling our lives. He described the paths that lay before us, and the types of people we were likely to encounter.

While there were no reliable statistics available, it was clear that human trafficking in Vietnam was a vast and growing trade, with thousands – if not tens of thousands – of victims every year. It was a monstrous industry that took many forms, from boys and girls locked inside sweatshops within Vietnam itself, to girls and women forced into prostitution and marriage in China.

I learned that the vast majority of victims were taken by deception, rather than force. The trafficker would build a relationship with the target over a period of days, weeks, or months, gradually earning their trust before finally leading them away.

Michael cited a recent case where a girl had been trafficked by a young man she'd been dating for an entire year. Blue Dragon later discovered that the man had been dating five or six girls at the same time, grooming each of them for trafficking.

The traffickers had to be clever. If a victim was able to return home and make a statement to the police, the trafficker could be identified, and could potentially face ten to twenty years in prison.

"The trafficker is assuming that the girl will never come back to Vietnam, that she will die in China," said Michael. "That's a really brutal approach that these traffickers have. They are gambling their own lives on the bet that this girl will die, rather than come home."

Vietnam's ethnic minority groups – and particularly those living in remote areas – tended to be poor, and poorly educated. They often had little understanding of human trafficking, little access to the law, and their poverty left them especially vulnerable to the promises traffickers used to lure their victims. A victim's parents might not speak any Vietnamese, and might not even have any papers or photographs to identify a kidnapped daughter to the authorities.

These groups were ideal targets, and were hit hardest by traffickers.

"From the traffickers' point of view, you want people who have no contacts, no recourse, and can't do anything about it," Michael told me. "That's why rural people are more likely targets, that's why ethnic minority people are more likely targets, and it's why impoverished girls are the lowest on the food chain."

It was easy to see why so many Hmong girls were being taken from the streets of Sapa – and, being so close to the Chinese border, there was precious little time for the authorities to respond before the girls were spirited out of the country.

There were numerous trafficking rings operating in the northern mountains – some were larger, transnational mafias, while others were smaller and more opportunistic. I'd assumed the trade relied on corrupt border officials turning a blind eye, but Michael said that was unnecessary, and generally unlikely.

"There are quite a few provinces that share a border with China," he said. "Often they're remote, they're mountainous, and therefore very hard to police."

There were many ways to get past the guards, along trails in unmarked areas of the border; a victim might not even realise she'd left Vietnam until it was far behind her.

Once across the border, a girl could be taken anywhere in China. Blue Dragon had rescued many girls who had been trafficked into brothels along China's southern coast, a popular sex-tourism destination for Chinese men. Some girls were sold thousands of kilometres from home.

By that time, Blue Dragon had rescued more than eighty girls from China, the vast majority of whom had been sold into brothels. Only two of the rescued girls had been forced into marriage – including my friend Vu.

Two years earlier, with very limited information, two of Blue Dragon's operatives had entered China in an attempt to locate and rescue both May and Vu. They'd succeeded in finding Vu, and had brought her home safely – but there just hadn't been enough information to find May. They hadn't even been able to learn which region of China she was in. It was the only time Blue Dragon had ever returned to Vietnam without the girl they'd been hoping to rescue.

"So the case went cold," said Michael. "But it looks like it's back on."

THE GENERAL CALLING

I'd received May and Pang's Chinese phone numbers from Zao, and passed them to Michael. I hadn't tried to call either of the numbers, and had no intention of doing so. I understood that it was a delicate situation, and that Blue Dragon would now have to proceed very carefully.

I asked Michael what the next step would be in handling May's case.

"She's made a telephone call," he said. "We need to investigate who she's contacted and what their relationship is. There's a lot of groundwork that goes on even before we reach out, because the cost of making a mistake is too high."

To my surprise, Zao had told me that Pang was happy in China. Michael was very wary of accepting such a statement at face value.

"We have to investigate," he said. "Even if we get the message saying, 'I'm married, I have children, and I don't want to come back to Vietnam', that's something we'd have to confirm ten times to be absolutely sure. It's a case of doubt everything, and question everything, until there can be no more room for doubt – because somebody's life here is now in our hands."

When I asked him to elaborate, Michael explained that even the simplest statements could hide a complex psychological reality.

"The girls often have a sense of guilt and shame, so whatever she says now we have to question: Is that what she really means, or is it what she thinks we want to hear, or is it what she thinks she deserves? She might be in China, desperate to come back, and she might say to you, 'No, I'm happy here'. She may not know herself at this point – she's been gone a long time."

Rescuing a girl was a long and delicate process and, at every step, Michael emphasised the importance of safety – for the sake of both the girl and the team. Unless there was a real emergency, it was best to proceed slowly.

"Until the girl is safe back home, anything is a possibility," he said. "She could be in a brothel. She could be happily married with no intention of returning to Vietnam. At those early stages of the investigation, you can't narrow yourself down to thinking you know what's going on – even if she's saying, this is what's happened, and this is what I want. You still have to hold open the possibility that there's more to the story. Otherwise, you're getting yourself into danger."

When Marinho and I left Blue Dragon that afternoon, I was buzzing with excitement. Michael had given me a far better understanding of what we were dealing with, and had given us an excellent interview for the documentary. With her Chinese number in hand and Blue Dragon on the case, there seemed to be a very strong chance that May would soon be coming home to her family in Vietnam.

Everything had fallen perfectly into place, and far more quickly than I'd imagined possible.

That evening, I checked my Facebook, and the floor fell out beneath me.

May's cousin Ha had shared May's phone number with all of her Facebook contacts, encouraging them to call May in China.

"Hello to everyone who knew May. I heard something about May. She is in China," Ha wrote. "If who would like to call her or try to help her escape from that place. You can try to call this phone number."

Hundreds of people around the world now had access to May's Chinese phone number. Like myself, many of those people were May's friends who knew she'd been abducted, would love to have a chance to help her, and would be delighted to speak to her again.

Few of those people would understand the complexities of May's situation. A single call from any one of them could jeopardise May's safety, and any chance of helping her. We didn't know how May had been able to access a phone, or if her captors knew she'd made contact with the outside world. If May was caught receiving international calls, we risked losing our only line of contact, and May herself could be in very real danger.

I remembered what Michael had told me only that morning: "If you mess up one of these cases, it could result in a girl being killed. It's that serious. If the trafficker knows that their victim has been communicating with someone in Vietnam, and calling for help, they may have to protect themselves by harming that girl. So we've got to make sure that nothing like that can happen."

It wasn't Ha's fault – it was mine. I'd understood the situation far better than she had, and kicked myself for not having explained how delicate it was.

After adding a comment urging people not to call May, I messaged Ha asking her to remove the number immediately, and waited impatiently for her response.

It wasn't until the following afternoon that Ha removed her message and wrote to apologise, saying she'd only wanted to help – but the damage had been done. Too many people now had access to May's number. We didn't know who might call it, when, or what the consequences might be for May.

When Blue Dragon began cautiously reaching out to May, they were able to make contact only once, and briefly. They struggled to understand what May was saying – and when they tried to call her again, the number no longer worked.

We'd lost her.

My investigation had already taken me much further than I'd dared hope. Now, thanks to my own carelessness, we'd lost the only chance we had to help May – perhaps the only chance we'd ever have.

Had May been harmed? Had I already ruined any hope of finding her?

I told myself that the outcome would have been the same if I hadn't been involved – but that didn't matter. I had been involved, and I'd failed to see the risk. We might never hear from May again, and might never know what had happened to her.

Having spent most of my adult life living and travelling around the world, I knew that every journey was life-changing. Yet I was just beginning to realise that this journey would go beyond anything I'd ever experienced, and change many more lives than just my own. It would affect friends and strangers in Vietnam, China, and around the world. It would reshape – and perhaps shatter – entire families.

I felt an enormous weight of responsibility upon me. For the first time, I was beginning to see what an emotionally complex and challenging journey it was to become – and I hadn't even reached Sapa yet.

It was there in Sapa that I'd meet resistance from three of the people whose support I'd most relied upon, and it was there that my resolve would be tested in ways I'd never imagined.

Even as I watched this strange new path unwind

beneath my feet, I couldn't guess what I might find around the next bend. I had no way of knowing to what dizzying heights and crushing depths it was yet to lead me.

COLD AS ICE

Once again, I took the night bus that wound its way up into the northern mountains – but the Sapa I found was not the one I had left.

The last time I'd seen Sapa, it had been August. The weather had been warm, the streets had been teeming with locals and foreigners, and the rice terraces had been lush and green before the annual harvest.

Now it was mid-January, and snow dusted the mountains. Sapa was bitterly cold, and its streets were almost empty. The rice terraces were bare and frosty, their muddy brown shelves stubbled with the broken stems of dead plants. The Hmong girls and women who had once swamped the town were few and far between.

There were backpackers arriving in Sapa in their shorts and flip-flops, utterly unprepared to find such brutally cold weather in the tropics. Only the most determined lingered in town; the rest quickly retreated to more comfortable altitudes.

The nights were close to freezing, with a damp chill that penetrated everything. Marinho and I holed up at the Yellow Dragon, with Toan, Huong, and their growing family. The rooms were unheated and we slept in all of our clothes, huddled beneath as many blankets as we could find.

I'd been five thousand metres above sea level amongst the highest mountains on Earth, and forty degrees below zero in the Canadian Rockies – but always with warmer clothing and better heating. There were few times in my life I could remember having been so cold.

I could hardly imagine how painful the nights must have been for the Hmong people living in their crude homes in the mountains around Sapa, with the icy winds whistling through the gaps in the walls. What a miserable time it must have been for the women who rose in the darkness before dawn to light their cooking fires with frozen fingers.

Toan was prospering as a husband, father, and manager of the Yellow Dragon's restaurant. While his new roles revealed a more responsible side to his character, he was still the same Toan I'd known three and a half years earlier, and it was wonderful to see him again.

Now that Huong had become a mother, I saw a gentler side to her, and a comfortable friendship replaced the tensions that had once stood between us.

I was delighted to meet Toan and Huong's growing family. Their daughter was now two years old, and their son was just three months.

I quickly realised that Toan was expecting me to play the same role I'd always played in Sapa: someone with plenty of free time, who was always ready to join him and his friends for a meal, a drink, or an adventure.

He was disappointed to learn that I would be working in Sapa, on a project which would take up nearly all of my time. I was sorry I couldn't tell Toan exactly why I'd come back to Sapa, but it was just too dangerous.

After my disastrous oversight in Hanoi, I understood Michael's emphasis on slow, deliberate action.

Marinho and I would have to move very carefully, and couldn't tell anyone in Sapa what we were doing – not even Toan, who had been like a brother to me. He might easily have one drink too many and let a careless word slip in the wrong company, and we simply couldn't take that risk.

LEARNING THE GAME

Sapa was a small town where rumours travelled quickly, and I knew that the traffickers were very close. They walked the same streets I walked, and spoke to the same people I spoke to. This small town I'd once called home had become the setting for a ruthless game, in which countless lives were at stake.

It was not a game with fixed rules: it was an evolution, mirroring a natural evolution between predators and their prey. As the Hmong girls of Sapa gradually learned to protect themselves against each new form of attack, the traffickers developed new methods of hunting them, and discovered new weaknesses to exploit.

The traffickers were typically young men of the girls' own culture, usually a few years older than the girls they preyed upon. They came from other Hmong communities scattered along both sides of the border.

Because they were strangers in Sapa, they could easily give false names, and lie about the locations of their homes and families.

In 2010 – when I'd first lived in Sapa – there had been relatively few disappearances there, and the kidnappers' strategies had been simple. Under some flimsy pretext, a young man could invite a girl he barely knew across the border – to attend a cousin's wedding in China, for example, or to visit some of his friends.

The girls hadn't yet seen the traps being laid for them, and had little reason to be suspicious. The invitation might have seemed a sign of romantic interest, or just a fun and harmless adventure.

Most of those girls had never come back.

In 2011, there was a dramatic increase in the number of girls being abducted from Sapa. May and Pang had both been taken that year. With their friends disappearing, the girls who remained behind became increasingly wary of such invitations.

A trafficker then had to spend more time in Sapa building trust with a girl, typically making promises of love and marriage. All he needed was enough trust for his target to climb onto the back of his motorbike, and he could spirit her away. He'd keep his victim unaware of their true destination until it was too late for her to do anything about it.

This kind of kidnapping took a greater investment of time and energy from the trafficker, and exposed him to greater danger. He was forced to spend more time in

Sapa with the girl, and risked being identified by her friends and family if he ever returned there.

After snatching their victims, the traffickers rarely returned to Sapa, presumably moving on to fresh hunting grounds in other towns and villages.

As more and more girls were taken from Sapa, it became increasingly difficult for the traffickers to get close to their prey. Girls became ever-more suspicious of unfamiliar young men, and relied on their friends to vouch for any newcomers.

In response, the traffickers devised a new trick, taking advantage of the region's desperate poverty. They began offering a share of their profits to local contacts within the communities they were feeding upon.

These insiders would introduce the traffickers to potential targets amongst their own friends and families. They vouched for the traffickers, helping to build the trust they needed to get close to their victims.

It was a masterful tactic, and there were now more girls disappearing from Sapa than ever before.

While the traffickers themselves were generally young men from out of town, these insiders could be anyone – young or old, male or female, a friend or a family member of the victim.

Girls were being sold down the river by people they'd known their whole lives – people they trusted, and perhaps even loved. These insiders were otherwise ordinary people whose crimes and connections made them desperate and dangerous.

I quickly learned that May, Pang, and Vu were not the only girls I'd known who had been kidnapped from Sapa. May's sister Cho, and another of their friends, had also been taken.

For so many girls to have disappeared from the same group, I was sure that someone very close must be working with the traffickers – but who?

I'd lived in Sapa for three months, three and a half years ago. I considered the Hmong girls my friends, but there were huge gaps between us – in age, culture, and life experience. How well did I really know these girls, what their lives were like, or what they were truly capable of?

The girls in Sapa no longer knew who to trust, and neither did I. I had to find the insider who had betrayed May and her friends to the traffickers, before they found me. There was no saying what that person might do to protect themselves when their lucrative game was threatened and they faced time in prison.

Until the insider was caught, my other friends remained in danger, and so did I.

It was difficult to believe that someone I knew had betrayed so many of her friends to the traffickers, and might do so again at any time. It was easier to tell myself that I was just being paranoid – but I wasn't.

Over the coming months, my suspicions proved correct. Someone from May's inner circle had indeed been working with the traffickers.

By the time I was able to confirm her identity, she

already knew exactly what I was doing there in Sapa, and was already one step ahead of me.

A MESSAGE FROM MICHAEL BROSOWSKI

Founder of Blue Dragon Children's Foundation

Every week, I receive emails from people all around the world wanting to get involved and help end human trafficking.

People want to know what they can do, and most of the time the only answer is to donate money. That money pays the salaries of people who rescue girls from trafficking, and pays for the accommodation, hospital bills, and food that is essential to their recovery.

When Ben Randall emailed, I could see that something was different. Ben wasn't looking to donate – he had a vision and a plan already. He was going to find his friends who were being held in slavery, and he was going to document his search so that the world could see the cruel reality of human trafficking.

For him, this was personal.

May and Pang are incredibly fortunate that they had a friend in Ben who cared enough to put all his time and resources into finding them. Blue Dragon Children's Foundation also sees that the rescue and care of every girl, boy, woman and man who has been enslaved and exploited is something personal.

At the time that Ben's astonishing documentary is being released, we have rescued around 900 trafficked people, of all ages, from brothels, sweatshops, street gangs and forced marriages. How have we done so?

Simply put: one at a time.

We have to see it this way, because the facts and the data are overwhelming. The most quoted figures say that right now, up to 45 million people in our world live in slavery, and no country is exempt from this scourge.

But the data does not tell the whole story. Arguably, it tells us very little. The numbers are all estimates, and all dependent on so many variables that they can't possibly be accurate.

What they do tell us, though, loud and clear, is that human trafficking is a massive global problem and demands a massive global response.

Blue Dragon's first rescue of a sex trafficking victim across the border in China was of a girl I will call "Nan" in 2007. Prior to that, we had been helping street children and rescuing children taken from rural areas into sweatshops within Vietnam. We had not set out to get involved in cross-border rescues, but a call for help came from a 16 year old girl we knew through our centre for street children in Hanoi. She called from a payphone telling a friend that she was in China, didn't know exactly where, and begged for help before the line was dead.

That was all the information we had. It seemed impossible that we – or anyone – would ever find Nan. But we did, and we brought her back to Vietnam along with five other Vietnamese girls and young women who had been tricked by traffickers into going to China on a 'holiday', and were instead sold to a brothel.

Our first cross-border rescue was close to being our last. We hadn't intended to actually conduct a rescue; we simply wanted to know where Nan was so we could report to the police. Once we were there and found Nan, the situation escalated almost immediately: the traffickers spotted us and attacked. It was a terrifying incident. Although we ultimately were successful in bringing Nan and the other young women home – and having the traffickers arrested – we vowed we would never do another such operation.

And for three years, we didn't. But when another call for help came, from three young women trapped in China and about to be sold to brothels, we had to go back and help.

Rescue work is often dangerous, but it is critical in the fight against slavery. Blue Dragon only rescues people who have identified that they wish to be helped, and we continue supporting them long after the rescue – through schooling, safe housing, psychological counselling, and legal advocacy.

A philanthropist friend of mine, Marc Gold, once told me about the time he met Mother Teresa. He said to her that he felt overwhelmed by all the world's needs, and didn't know where to start. She responded by asking what he would do if he was standing on the shore of a beach and could see an overturned ship off the coast, with many people drowning and calling for help. Marc replied that he would swim out there to try to at least save someone, to which Mother Teresa promptly told him: "So start swimming."

This is what Ben Randall has done, and what our whole world needs to do, if we are to bring an end to human trafficking. The whole world agrees that this terrible crime must stop – and that's possible, if we all work together to make it happen.

A SPECIAL PREVIEW OF
SUSPICIOUS MINDS

PART TWO OF THE INCREDIBLE
TRUE STORY BEHIND THE ACCLAIMED
'SISTERS FOR SALE' DOCUMENTARY

GHOST TOWN

Three and a half years after my departure from Sapa, I returned to that realm of mist and fog nestled amongst Vietnam's northern mountains.

The first time I'd come to Sapa was in May 2010. I'd arrived there on holidays, as a backpacker. Sapa was supposed to be a brief stop on a three-year journey through Asia – until, almost by accident, it had become my home.

It was in Sapa that I'd first met the Black Hmong people, an impoverished tribal group struggling to survive in the rugged borderlands between Vietnam and China.

The Vietnamese Hmong people lived in a world of ghosts and monsters. They believed in shapeshifters, invisible things, and hairy little devils that herded tigers in the forest. They warned each other against tall, silent creatures that would rise from rivers to seize noisy children, beasts that sucked the blood of pigs, and the deranged woman with dog's teeth who devoured unattended babies.

It was incredible how little attention the Hmong people seemed to give to the true monster in their midst. Each year, many dozens of their sisters and daughters were being snatched and stolen away, to be sold to strangers in distant lands.

Sapa was in the throes of a major human trafficking crisis – and the strongest response from the local community seemed to be shaming and blaming the victims.

While I'd lived in Sapa, there had been a group of ten teenage Hmong girls who often sat on the corner of my street, selling handicrafts to tourists. We laughed and joked together every day – and, in time, I became friends with several of them.

Within twenty months of my departure from Sapa, no less than five of those ten girls were kidnapped in separate incidents.

There was one girl in particular who had always been the centre of attention, and had become my closest friend in the group: a tiny fourteen-year-old named May, who had a big smile, a big mouth, and a big heart.

It was now January 2014 – two and a half years since May's mysterious disappearance. I was returning to Sapa to find out what had happened to her: but I quickly realised that Sapa was a very strange place to search for the truth.

Sapa was a viper's nest of rumours. I was amazed how difficult it was to establish even the most basic facts in this world of superstition, gossip, and small-town intrigue.

Almost everyone in Sapa seemed to have a secret, or a hidden motive; it might be something innocent, or it could be something far more sinister. The locals were scared – of the traffickers, of the authorities, and of each other. Every time I heard a story it changed, often dramatically, and truth was entangled with fantasy. I had to sift through myriad distortions, lies, and rumours to get at the bare facts beneath.

The Hmong people had a very fluid sense of time and place, and often lost track of days, months, and years. There were no maps or calendars here, and few people could read or write. Apart from an occasional yellowing document, or a handful of old photographs tacked to a wall or tucked away in a purse, the only way to access the past was through memory. It was impossible to find out exactly when my friends had been kidnapped, or even when they'd been born.

As one friend put it, "Hmong people don't count. We don't have birthdays. People don't know how old they are, they're just guessing."

Someone might tell me, with absolute certainty, that May had been kidnapped in July – only to change their mind a moment later and assure me it was, in fact, August. When I asked which day of the week she'd been taken, I got answers like, "maybe Tuesday or Saturday".

Officially, the Vietnamese used the Gregorian calendar, as did most of the world – but they were also influenced by the Chinese calendar, which was based on the cycles of the sun and the moon.

In the villages outside Sapa, however, the sense of time was tied to the seasons: the planting season, the warm rainy season, the harvest, and the brutally cold winter. These were the hazy landmarks the local people used to orient themselves in time.

It could be incredibly difficult to tell who was related to whom, and how. The locals referred to distant relatives as cousins, to cousins as sisters and brothers, and to family friends as aunts and uncles. There was a rumour that May's family was not her real family, that they'd actually bought her as a child.

There were intense jealousies and rivalries even between close friends. I struggled to read people's true emotions, and to understand why they laughed at tragedies that tore families apart. Terrible truths lay concealed in vague expressions.

If a girl disappeared, it was often assumed with shocking rapidity that she had "gone to China", where she was beyond the reach of anyone who might want to help her.

The facts my Hmong friends related were further distorted by their erratic use of the English language. They struggled to describe certain things, and would often invent or substitute words. More complex ideas could easily become lost or confused. My friends would muddle their past, present, and future tenses, wreathing their stories in a fog of uncertainty.

I was accompanied in Sapa by a European cameraperson, Marinho, who was recording my investigations for a documentary we were producing. I interviewed dozens of people, both on and off camera, to learn all I could about the local human trafficking crisis, and quickly realised that the puzzle was far more complex than I could have imagined. Some of the pieces took months to fall into place, while others will never be found.

Many of the Hmong people shared the same names, and others were confusingly similar. Many were known by different names to different people. Just among the people involved in my investigation, there were Chu, Chu, Khu, Khu, Zu, Giu, Vu, Vu, Shu, Sho, Cho, Cho, Chan, Chinh, Chinh, Dinh, Dinh, Phinh, Pang, Pang, Cang, Lung, Dung, Ha, Ta, Xa, Xa, Xay, Nay, May, May, May, My, Zy, Zao, Zao, and Bao.

As I plunged ever-deeper into the swirling, ever-shifting labyrinth of lies and rumours, I realised there was just one piece of concrete information in Sapa that could give me any real hope of ever finding May.

That information was being jealously guarded by May's own father – and, as my investigation pushed forward, he was to do everything in his power to stop me from getting it.

Before my work was over, May's family was

threatening to have me killed for trying to help their daughter.

I wasn't on holidays anymore.

Order 'Suspicious Minds' now
and make a difference at
www.sistersforsale.com

ACKNOWLEDGEMENTS

Thank you so much to all of you who have supported and encouraged me during the creation of this book – especially my family.

A very special thank you to Dr. Michelle Imison and Brittnay Mayhue for their meticulous revisions and corrections, Sifis Zervoudakis for his insights, and Michael Brosowski for his wonderful contribution.

Thanks also to Mary Rennie for giving me a push, Jane Novak for being part of the journey, Katie Carriero for watching over 'The Human, Earth Project', Melissa Adams for her assistance with the website, and Astrid Hofer for managing our social media.

Last but certainly not least, a huge thank you to everyone who played a role in this story and made it possible. Some of you are named in the text, and some are not – you know who you are.

Part two of the incredible true story behind the acclaimed 'Sisters for Sale' documentary

SUSPICIOUS MINDS

BY BEN RANDALL

As teenage girls are being kidnapped from the streets of Sapa, an Australian filmmaker enters a labyrinth of lies and deception in search of the truth about his missing friends, May and Pang.

Hidden somewhere in May and Pang's inner circle, among the only people who can help find the missing girls, is the traitor who betrayed her friends to the traffickers - but who is it?

Learn more at www.sistersforsale.com

ISBN: 978-0-6487573-4-4 (paperback),
978-0-6487573-3-7 (PDF), 978-0-6487573-5-1 (epub)

Part three of the incredible true story behind the acclaimed 'Sisters for Sale' documentary

THE MAN'S MACHINE

BY BEN RANDALL

An Australian filmmaker struggles to find his kidnapped friends May and Pang in the immensity of China, where they have been forced into marriage with local men.

With his two-man team rapidly falling apart and a near-impossible time limit, he discovers a strange web of hidden connections leading back to May's family in Vietnam.

Learn more at www.sistersforsale.com

ISBN: 978-0-6487573-7-5 (paperback),
978-0-6487573-6-8 (PDF), 978-0-6487573-8-2 (epub)